STEVE   ı ıER

THE LAST DOG
ON
THE ISLAND

Tasmania's border protection heroine

NEW
HOLLAND

CONTENTS

Chapter 1.   **Initiating Stimulus** - 5

Chapter 2.   **Patience, Praise and Correction** - 17

Chapter 3.   **Search Patterns** - 35

Chapter 4.   **Directing Low and High** - 49

Chapter 5.   **The Handler is a Dog's Greatest Limitation** - 65

Chapter 6.   **Change in Behaviour** - 79

Chapter 7.   **Methods of Concealment** - 99

Chapter 8.   **Unconscious Cues** - 121

Chapter 9.   **Olfactory Acuity** - 139

Chapter 10.   **Target Odours** - 157

Chapter 11.   **Have Dog, Will Travel** - 175

Chapter 12.   **The Big Score** - 201

Chapter 13.   **The Last Parade** - 213

Postscript - 218

Glossary - 219

CHAPTER 1

INITIATING STIMULUS

The Detector Dog Training Centre manager looked at me for a few long seconds before speaking.

'Tasmania is an odd place and it takes a particular kind of person to make it work there … but I think we have chosen well,' he concluded.

I could but hope he was right.

First day on the island

The sleeper cabin on the overnight ferry to Devonport was more comfortable than the accommodation I had enjoyed on my previous voyages as a tourist. On my holidays the year before I had paid for a seat only and, hidden at the far end of the top deck, had dozed fitfully in my sleeping bag as the ship rolled and pitched, dimly aware of the footsteps and chatter of passing crew members.

Leaving an overcast Melbourne, I arrived in the new land. Sunlight bathed the white lighthouse standing sentinel over a country town's early calm. Behind it, the dark dorsal fin of dramatic bluffs rose high in silhouette to the west.

The road took me south to a new home in Hobart, a new town and a new state. My life had turned full circle and I was going back to working as a Customs dog handler, reprising a job I had taken up 18 years previously. Actually, not 'a', but rather 'the' handler for the Southern-most state. The rumour in Customs was that management were thinking of phasing out the Tasmanian Detector Dog Unit position, and that the next Customs dog to go there would be the last dog on the island.

I was moving because I needed a change and because I had run out of ideas about what to do with my life after returning from South America six months previously. My life had hit a wall and I was dying to get off the treadmill of shift work at Melbourne airport. The last straw had been a ranger position I wanted and couldn't get.

There was more than a hint of self exile involved – hiding my wastrel life from the gaze of those I knew and loved. I was leaving my family behind in Melbourne. Meredith, my girlfriend, and I were facing the uncertainty of a long-distance relationship and considering the possibility of her moving to Tasmania.

The sole dog handler's job in Tasmania was vacant. Customs was struggling to find anyone experienced who wanted to move there. It was an exit, actually my only exit, other than resigning. Even though handling dogs had been a job I had once loved, I pondered the wisdom of going back. However, working elsewhere had reinforced a lesson I had learned early – working with dogs beat the hell out of working with people.

•••

What would a foreigner make of this island? The mountains and forests which dominate the small towns make it look as if nature is pushing the settlements into the sea, but once here one soon sees that it is the other way around. The stream of logging trucks headed for the woodchip piles at the seaport suggest that the towns are pushing the forests into the sea.

Road signs provide tantalising and bizarre suggestions as to the quirks of life in Tasmania.

'Food, fun and ferrets', a combination found nowhere else in the world. The Axeman's Hall of Fame, hopefully a temple to the sport of country shows, rather than to the state's grim convict origins.

Metal cut-outs of the Tasmanian emu and Tasmanian tigers (a now-extinct type of marsupial wolf) appear beside the road. The smattering of holes in the figures show that the metal varieties are no more bullet proof than the originals.

Opium poppies swaying in the wind, the green bulbs shimmering in the sun. Apparently, it's not so hard to find drugs here.

The bare plains of the central midlands, cleared of trees by over-zealous pioneers, and now subject to troubling erosion, dotted with signs announcing control works that do not seem to include planting trees.

•••

Onward to Hobart, where even the poorest suburbs had a water view. A quick drive through the few traffic lights took me to my hotel. My new home, until I found something more permanent, was in Battery Point surrounded by cottages, the English-village atmosphere laid on thick under the green slopes of Mount Wellington.

My life with a dog

After being a Customs dog handler for 10 years in Melbourne between 1987 and 1997, I had left the Melbourne Detector Dog Unit (DDU) not under a cloud, but rather on one. I had turned 30, finished my park management degree, and had taken a years' long service leave to see the world, hoping to then start a new career as a park ranger.

I was crying when I left, my voice shaking during my farewell speech to the dog unit. Saying goodbye to Detector Dog (DD) Spinner was my last act, going down to his kennel alone, hugging him with tears coursing down my face as I said goodbye to a job that I had truly loved and put my heart and soul into. But it was time to leave.

I believed, optimistically it turned out, that within a year of returning from leave I would be in a ranger's job somewhere, and thus was prepared to put up with shift work and the endless lines of passengers through Melbourne airport. I must have written over a hundred applications to park agencies in every state, and performed hundreds, possibly thousands of hours of volunteer work for Parks Victoria, friends' groups and Conservation Volunteers.

Eight years later, the only changes to my circumstances were self-induced. Long stretches of leave to escape the monotony of the airport and shift work, travelling the world in search of adventure, escaping my disappointment and confusion about what to do next.

I was awarded the position as Tasmanian handler not on the basis of the one-line email I wrote as my application, but because of my 10 years experience as a dog handler in Melbourne. I had learned about handling through my many mistakes, training four dogs with very different temperaments. I had some limited successes and some humbling failures. I was now turning 40 after living a prolonged adolescence.

Before I could go to Tasmania, I had to go back to the Canberra Customs Detector Dog Training Centre (DDTC) again, where all dogs and handlers were trained. My retraining was the part of the deal that I felt least prepared for and where I knew I would probably be found most wanting. I remembered the training was tough on a 20-year-old – as someone who was nearly 40 I thought that it might be beyond my capacity.

I had graduated from my first course in 1987 with DD Shadow, a short-haired German Shepherd who lasted all of three weeks due to chronic hip dysplasia making the effort of jumping too painful for him. It is a common physical defect in Shepherds, resulting from too much inbreeding and the resultant magnification of genetic problems. The dog's hip problem should have been picked up in training – it meant a false start to my career as a dog handler.

I was sent DD Blitzen a few months later. His handler had left after disputes with management. Blitzen was a striking semi-long-haired Shepherd with yellow eyes like a big cat, and an impressive mane and voluminous coat that required much care and grooming. I handled Blitzen for three years, at the end of which he was returned due to mental instability and pronounced mood swings.

In terms of his performance, I had made the rookie mistake of being too single-minded about his training. This meant he became too attuned to my patterns, odour and looking for training items rather than the unexpected nature of real drug concealments.

I spent six months searching ships with the Shipping Enforcement group while waiting for another dog to become available.

I was then able to put the hard lessons learned from the mistakes I had made with Blitzen to constructive use with DD Oscar. Oscar was a boisterously good-natured gold Labrador, ex-Brisbane. Customs was dealing solely with these medium-sized, people-friendly and robust working dogs, and no longer recruiting German Shepherds.

Oscar was my most successful dog in Melbourne and I dedicated a great amount of youthful energy to working him – the sort of energy I could no longer muster after years of shift work and bouts of glandular fever and chronic fatigue. We achieved the Melbourne record of 201 drug seizures in two years, although most of them were only relatively small amounts in mail, premises searches and in baggage on domestic flights.

Oscar did have a singular and remarkable ability to locate heroin buried in the ground, no matter how heavily contained or small the amount, pinpointing three caches in inexplicably difficult circumstances. These canine triumphs surpassed my expectations and were a surprise to the police and the criminals involved. They also reinforced my belief in being a dog handler – being a good team could make a difference. Elise, my Narcotic Detector Dog for Tasmania, was to validate my faith in the value of being a team.

Oscar was also getting on in years, having had at least two handlers before me. Customs Dogs are usually retired between eight and ten years old and although his ability was undaunted, he had reached retirement age and it was time for me to get another dog.

DD Spinner was a long-limbed Labrador who had had had a short and chequered career with his previous handler. After a few months of training problems, the handler had decided that the DDU wasn't for him and left his problem child with us.

I used to call Spinner a 'bloody nuisance of dog'. He was always attempting to wind up the other dogs with his barking and behaviour. I once watched Spinner tear off a branch from a gum sapling and, gripping it in his teeth, thrust it through the cyclone wire at another dog, teasing it while it snapped and threw itself against the fence.

He also had a habit of jumping against the yard gate just as someone was closing it, causing the metal gate to collide with that person's head as he or she bent over to close the catch. I soon got even with him by suddenly swinging the gate inward as he jumped, knocking him over and ensuring that he didn't try it again with me.

'Well, he's my bloody nuisance of a dog now,' I thought as I set myself to adjusting to working with him after sending my much beloved Oscar home to live with my parents.

In a few months, Spinner had stopped being a biting, barking beast and had turned into a much calmer dog. I quickly found that it had been his last handler's influence that had encouraged the poor behaviour, and Spinner soon developed into an excellent worker. We soon achieved seizures of cocaine, steroids and hashish concealed in vacuum cylinders from Thailand.

Spinner marked our improved cohesion as a team with some more drug seizures – he had gone from being a nuisance to being an asset.

International express mail from places like Thailand and Brazil usually received the full treatment from the dog unit, the bags opened and parcels laid out in lines to obtain good access before they were x-rayed and screened by postal officers. We were looking for heroin and cocaine and needed to get the dogs' noses on the parcels to improve our chances of finding concealed drugs.

I had some modest success with Oscar flicking his head – nothing more that a hesitation of his nose as he passed over them – on a number of flat envelopes from Thailand supposed to contain documents. We found an ounce of heroin in each compressed flat between layers of carbon paper.

Spinner moved a little out of his target odour range, showing a sustained interest in five large parcels from Bangkok the contents of which were described as chocolates. Thailand is not known for chocolate production – the climate is rather too hot for chocolate to keep. Inside each box was a large sealed tin of European chocolate, and under the first layer a bag of multi-coloured pills like a pharmacy. They didn't look like 'ecstasy' pills with their trademark colours and logos, and turned out to be steroids.

Not in the same league as heroin, but at least we were getting close. The strong chemical odour had attracted

Spinner's attention while he tried to decide whether the pills were one of his target odours. That is how many seizures are made, a combination of the work of dog and handler.

Pasear al perro (walking the dog) — training in Canberra, again

When I returned to Canberra, my memories of arriving there as an anxious 20-year-old in 1987 came flooding back, perhaps to remind me of how little I had changed.

The echoing rasp of barking dogs, the stale-biscuit smell of dog food mixed with the sharp, revolting tang of disinfectant, green dog shit and the Easter Show odour of new leather. The barren, paw-scratched yards and straggling, much pissed-upon gums were the same, 17 years later.

I knew I was going to find it physically tough and wasn't looking forward to living in a motel room for three months in our bland capital. Worse, I was far from the ideal age to endure the endless, lung-searing and knee-pounding training runs. The DDU course is designed to train dogs and handlers from scratch, simultaneously, with the handlers learning as they and their dogs are taken through the process of detection training. The humans are always way behind the dogs because we are trying to learn something — the dogs are merely being channelled into something that is in their nature. Dogs use their sense of smell constantly for finding food, marking territory or telling friends from enemies and have an enlarged area in their brains (the olfactory lobe) as well as many millions of times more nasal receptor cells than humans which enable them to do so.

It is estimated that in terms of behaviour, around 80 per cent of a dog's behaviour is innate (genetic) and about 20 per cent is learned after birth. For humans, the proportions are approximately the opposite – 80 per cent learned and 20 per cent innate.

My recollection of training in Canberra was of long, hot days crouched in the diminishing shade of a dog trailer parked in bleached paddocks, returning reluctant dogs to their cages, their tongues lolling and my chest heaving. This was after zigzag sprints as the hounds chased the zephyr scent of drugs from their hiding spots somewhere in the Canberra bush, all accompanied by the curses and disapproval of our ill-tempered and large-moustached instructor burning in my ears. My cracked and aching hands struggling with the sharp metal catches of the trailer doors, the box shaking with the headlong rushes of the next dog to be released.

The dogs had been a mixture of pound strays, donated 'bitsers' and failed police dogs. There were cattle dogs, Weimaraners, crazy-eyed Shepherds and others of parentage too difficult to divine. Now all the dogs are Labradors in a choice of three colours – gold, black or brown. Some are calm, some frenetic, but all are bred and raised to be manic retrievers.

My throat was nightclub raw from shouting encouragement, hands speckled with punctures from unintended bites and leg muscles piano-string taut from trying to keep up with young dogs running at rabbit-chasing speed as well as fitness runs three times a week.

While a gallery of instructors, admin and kennel staff watched me trying to call back a happy Labrador bitch, I felt as if I had forgotten what I had learned during my ten years of handling dogs for Customs and only remembered the early humiliation of the training centre.

There were so many elements to remember and so little time and space to fit them all in. Pivot, command and hand signal. Get on your bike! Second hand signal, shorten the lead. Don't crowd the dog – watch him! Change hands reverse pattern. Command and hand signal. Straighten up, give some lead. Shorten up. Get ahead. Bring him round. Give it space … wait … Good boy! With legs feeling like lead and self-confidence sinking, I knew that my body was struggling and my heart wasn't really in this decision to take my life full circle. I was wondering whether it was better to admit as much and quit or to go ahead out of pride and leave afterwards.

CHAPTER 2

PATIENCE, PRAISE AND CORRECTION

Dog training 101

Stories about 'sniffer dogs' are frequently in the media, especially given the current security climate that the media like to harp on. There are stories about dogs being used to detect potential suicide bombers on public transport, failing to find test explosives at airports, being used to intimidate people, to screen for drugs at music concerts or in schools, to detect signs of cancer or smuggled birds and so on.

There is much information and misinformation about them, much unqualified opinion given and few facts about how detector dogs are trained, how they work and what they can and can't do. I want to provide some information as a balance to all the myth and mystique. I can't give details about detecting explosives, or cancers, or cadavers, because I have only ever trained dogs to find drugs, but the principle is the same, no matter what the smell.

A dog is not an Inspector Rex, a super-cop on four legs. Dogs are as reliable and as flawed as human beings, but not as complex. They have the same limitations as any of the machines invented to do the same job, but are much more portable and friendly. Dogs are not the only means of finding drugs, bombs or any other odour, but isn't it curious, given our technology-driven world, that dogs are still used in ever increasing numbers for these tasks? It says much about the limitations of computers.

Australian Customs (now Australian Border Force) trains Labrador dogs to find drugs, explosives and firearms, chemical weapon precursors and cash. They are all trained on the same basis, regardless of the smell they are trained to find. Let's deal with the myth about dogs having to be drug addicts to find drugs. All of the dogs are superbly fit and healthy. None of them is addicted to drugs. None of them eat explosives, snort anthrax or smoke grass rolled in $100 notes.

A happy Labrador pup is encouraged from the age of a few months to play a hunting game of sniffing out a favourite toy from under a line of upturned plant pots. The puppy is given time to play with the toy and lots of praise when it finds it. This is basically what the dog is trained to do as an adult, except the hunt may be in a cargo shed full of boxes, a busy airport terminal teeming with people, on the rusty deck of a cargo ship or a moving belt conveying luggage or mail parcels. The game is to find one of those special smells and to indicate where it is coming from. The handler will give the dog its favourite toy and lots of play in return.

That's the short version – the concept in a nutshell. Getting from the puppy in the backyard to the dog seeking in a crowded airport takes quite a few more steps, and keeping them seeking a few more. This story is a walk along that path.

The National Training Centre (then in Canberra and now in Melbourne) takes dogs from just beyond their puppy stage and trainee handlers and introduces them both to the process of scent association. The dogs and the humans are learning concurrently. The dogs usually catch on faster than the humans. The dog is first imprinted with the odours it needs to find by scenting 'dummies' – pieces of hand towel rolled up to make a cylinder – with the target odour. Out in a Canberra park, the dummy, the dog's favourite toy, is waved and thrown while the handler tries to keep up and have some breath to play. At that moment, the dog receives the toy, its reward and its target odour. This is repeated for each odour the dog is to find. A drug detection dog, for instance, is trained on at least four different drug odours.

The training slowly becomes more sophisticated as the dummies and their associated target odours are hidden from the dog's view, so it has to use its nose to find the toy, rather than its eyes.

The target odours are then hidden in all the scenarios where the dogs are expected to search. The handler teaches the dog the best way to search around a room, in a car, cargo shed or baggage belt. When the dog has searched to find the target smell, located it and responded in the manner it has been shown, it receives the reward toy.

Of course, in a drug shipment there are no toys, so the handler keeps an unscented one to substitute (or 'sub') it when the dog indicates that it has found one of the target odours – the dog gets its toy and a game in return for carrying out its training.

After 2006, all Australian Customs dogs were trained to sit next to their target odours. They were previously trained to sit next to people and to scratch or bite any unaccompanied objects such as suitcases or boxes. Using dogs to search lines of passengers seems like an obvious thing to do, but it was not accepted until the late 90s that the dogs should be allowed to do this, and all the social and legal issues had to be dealt with.

The games people play

The tug of war game played with the dog as a reward for finding a target odour is really the most important motivator for the retrieving-obsessed animal. No reward and no game ultimately means no work from the dog. It is really the verbal input that is more demanding than the physical game, a constant monologue to try and make the game a happy and rewarding experience, rather than a grim struggle.

The dogs have different characteristics. Some are frenetic, some inscrutable, some steady, some love to jump, or lick faces or stretch up on their hind legs against you. Like people, no two dogs are the same, and the primary motivation of the tug of war game has to be individually tailored to the dog's likes.

The one-way conversation between handler and dog is the sort of babble that most people to keep between their pets and themselves – it's like being overheard talking to yourself.

When heard out of context, say by some person who doesn't

realise that it involves playing with a dog, the person talking sounds certifiable!

Good boy! Oh good boy that's a boy. Where'd you get that, eh? Good dog! What you got there matey? Get it … good boy! What a clever dog, best dog! Oh yes! Can I get that? Oooh good boy. Watch out, I'm going to get your dummy! Ah ha! I got it! Oh good boy, what a clever one! Want to run? That's mine now. Oh good boy!

It is accompanied by much patting and pantomime faces and movements, making swipes at the end of a rolled-up towel protruding form the dog's mouth, trying to not get one's hands bitten.

Part of the selection process for handlers is to find people who are not self conscious about volubly and physically playing the game with a dog in public. At the end of a long training run, or a long day of searching, the game can feel like too much effort to the handler. Searching may be important to humans, but for the dogs, the game is all they are working for.

The exercises teach dogs and handlers different search patterns for each scenario – a premises search, a cargo shed, a ship or the contents of mail bags.

The hardest thing to do is to keep a step ahead of the dog and anticipate their movements, taking action to bring the dog back into a line of search to ensure that areas or items aren't missed in the search. Trainee handlers also must learn to read all the environmental variables, such as the wind and air currents and their sources, to know how best to deploy a dog in a search and how to read what the dog is doing.

There is a lot of time between training exercises, waiting for the other handlers to perform and then for the instructors to set up the same exercise for the next dog, in order to gauge the dog's and your own ability against the same standard.

The highly-strung hounds restrained by a harness, pick their ears up at the sounds of unseen activity – we can only guess how it colours their minds. As much as we try to keep the sights and sounds of the success, or lack of it, from the next dog waiting in line for their turn at the training exercise, they hear the distant squeak of 'Good boy!' as surely as the distant howl of a hunting pack.

• • •

The dog listened while I stared at the sky, watching the yellow-tailed black cockatoos cracking pine cones and the flash of the rosellas against the blue. I repeated the mantra for the next lesson. Leash short, pump the second, fourth and sixth articles, slow up, shorten up and step to the left for the pivot. It was like some prayer that I hoped would get me through the next manic minute after the call 'OK!' came from inside the training hall. I also knew that the dog would do something I hadn't predicted.

• • •

I often felt guilty for all the wasted time that could have been spent thinking of something productive. It seemed that my intelligence was draining slowly from me as long as I lived a life of physical activity.

The waiting in Canberra hadn't changed, just the location.

We used to wait with the dog trailer out in the heat-hazed bush near Mount Ainslie, watching for the return of a panting dog and a sweat drenched trainee handler from a ridiculously long field run. The updated version involved holding the dog to the side of a corridor in Customs House, trying to keep out of the way of the office workers and listening for the sound of the previous dog being led away down the opposite corridor.

At first, the dogs were trained to actively respond to articles such as boxes and bags. After six weeks of digging and biting as a response they began the passive response training, where they were taught to search people and sit (passive response) when they smelt a drug odour.

This dual response (active/passive) training proved to be too confusing for them. Having been encouraged to tear into cardboard and to try and bite holes in suitcases, they were now firmly held by the collar and made to sit. Consequently, all the training was shifted to passive response only as it helped to get more dogs through training courses, especially those who had less aggressive tendencies.

To help acclimatise the dogs to working inside airports and searching lots of different people, the staff at Customs house were asked to volunteer their time and patience for dog training on a daily basis. They lined up against walls in offices and corridors, one usually strapped up with a quantity of drugs, playing the 'target'. On a good day, it probably provided the staff a diverting break from staring at computers, and on a bad one an unwelcome and noisy imposition on a deadline. The people lined up were all volunteers, but most of the unspoken disapproval came from the people we passed in the corridors, squeezed into a lift with while barely containing an excited Labrador, or unhappily surprised on the stairs or around a corner, while they edged away with expressions of distaste.

In Customs, dogs and the dog unit were something that you either loved or hated.

My course mates were representative of the states needing more dog handlers. Perth, Sydney and Brisbane. To fill in the hours of waiting in the vehicle for the next run to be set up and for the next team to take their turn, I had instituted reading aloud from the Readers Digest book of Mysteries, a book I had found being used as filling for a training suitcase.

The real mystery to the other trainees and staff was why I was back in Canberra on another handler course, putting myself through it all again. When asked, I would just smile and say I didn't know myself.

Ticker

I sat down beside the dog trailer parked in a scrap of shade at Russell, dabbing at a trickle of blood coming from above my ear. As a result of watching my dog and not where I was going, I had run with my head twisted around to follow the path of the dog's nose and collided with a locker mounted high on the workshop wall. Stunned, all I could think of was to get back ahead of my dog and direct it through the search pattern while warm drops tickled my eyebrows.

The training course instructor, might not have liked my handling style or attitude, but he lauded me for having 'ticker' (a strong heart) and not stopping the run. It was something ingrained in me that I had learned to endure on my first stint in Canberra in 1987. Then, the dogs were bigger and the bites were harder.

The German Shepherds were a different and in many ways, a more difficult dog to handle than the now favoured breed, the Labrador. Shepherds are particularly large and heavy. This made it difficult for many of the female handlers as it was required that handlers should be able to pick up and carry their dogs if necessary. When the dog weighed over 30 kg that took some strength. Also, in terms of personality, Shepherds are completely different and require a whole different style of handling and approach.

By and large the Shepherd is a much more serious and aloof dog and takes its role as shepherd, or guard of its master, very seriously. Generally, a Labrador takes the game to you, seeking your attention and affection, but with a Shepherd you must take the game to them, doing all the talking and encouragement. Meanwhile, the dog merely possesses the toy in its vice-like grip, never letting go and watching for your next move, using its size and weight against you. A game with a Shepherd is very dog focussed and not as much fun as the manic attention-seeking of the Labrador.

To be clear, when a Customs dog is corrected, it is never hit. They are verbally corrected with an 'easy!' if being guided on or a 'no!' if continuing would be detrimental to their training or health.

We used to teach the dogs basic obedience – heel, sit, stay, drop, come – but now it doesn't even extend to that, with the idea that committing the dog to any such action might distract them from following a drug odour. Sitting is now the passive response for finding a drug odour and hence is not used as obedience, and food is not used as a reward but as an environmental distraction which Customs dogs are taught to ignore.

I found out how vice-like the Shepherd grip actually was when 'subbing' on a drug-laden parcel in the demo hall of the Canberra training centre. I slammed down the dummy on the parcel, but trainee DD Shadow saw only the blur of movement and didn't wait to identify it, chomping down on my right hand and merrily shaking it up and down like a rabbit it his grasp. I gave an initial shout of surprise and was pulled to my knees with a couple of his canine teeth impaling my hand from each side. Somehow, I thought I should keep playing the game, lest I be marked down for my error, and murmured out a few 'good boys!' as I frantically searched for the dummy with my left hand. I threw it down on the parcel again, giving a relieved cry of praise when Shadow dropped my punctured hand.

It was all recorded on video and the calls of sympathy from the instructors and other handlers were audible. I received a rare mention in despatches for having enough 'ticker' to continue the game. I'm not sure if the dog knew it had my hand, and had now found another 'dummy' to play with, but there had been another time when a dog definitely knew it had the handler in its jaws.

I was at the Melbourne mail centre with another handler and his impressively boof-headed Shepherd, fittingly called 'Grip', when I heard the handler's chatter of tug of war talk turn to a sharp cry of pain.

I had been clearing up a line of parcels in the next aisle and raced around to find the handler on his knees, his face a mask of agony while Grip gleefully wrung his arm up and down like a rag doll. I raced forward waving the dummy from my pocket and calling for the dog's attention – a small distraction which Grip regarded briefly before resuming the torture. The handler's whitened fingers protruded from one side of Grip's mouth, pinched by a shark-like row of teeth. He was being pulled almost prone with his arm stretched out, yelling while Grip pulled back on his limb.

I saw then that Grip knew he had his handler's hand and was enjoying it. I threw myself around Grip's neck. Circling an arm around his throat and squeezing his windpipe in the crook of my elbow until he had to open his mouth to try to take a breath, I stayed on Grip, pressing him to the floor as he struggled to turn on me. In dog-fight terms, I had him by the throat, and he soon went limp in submission.

I grabbed him by the collar and firmly marched him back to the car, then drove rapidly to a surgery while my colleague nursed his crushed hand, which required five stitches.

As is the nature of the Shepherd, I had also seen those jaws used in defence of a handler.

On my first house raid in Melbourne, the AFP were having some ridiculous jaw-jutting, blokey argument with an eastern suburbs crook, in what was to become a familiar setting – a nice house, full of antiques and a flash car owned by someone getting the dole.

The dispute over the warrant erupted into a full shouting match in the kitchen while I was encouraging Shadow to search around the corridor. Suddenly, the suspect erupted into the doorway, effing and blinding and about to turn his ire on me. I recoiled in alarm and Shadow shot forward, launching himself at the man's face. Shadow only stopped when he reached the extent of the lead, his teeth clacking together audibly within a few centimetres of the man's nose. The guy fell back against the wall and crouched there, shaking. I hauled Shadow in and told the man to go back to the kitchen, with more authority than I felt. He nodded and turned away, shaking – as I was.

The personality issue with German Shepherds, and male Shepherds in particular, was that the handlers had to prove to the dog that they were the pack leader.

Every so often, about six months to a year or more, the dog would challenge your authority to be pack leader. It would begin with the dog getting slower in responding to commands, until it picked up its ears but didn't respond at all. When corrected, it curled its lips and growled. This was the challenge, and I had to be quick and firm in response. I grabbed the dog by the loose skin of its neck and hauled it off its feet, all its power gone, and screamed in its face. When I let it go, the dog wagged its submission and went immediately to heel. The battle was over for the next six months.

On the whole, I prefer the happy Labrador who looks to you for the next game and sign of affection.

The Alpha Male

Late in the piece another old hand at dog work who had come back to do a stint at the Canberra training centre joined the course. It was not some old handler returned to the fold due to lack of ambition and other prospects like myself – this veteran had four legs.

Alpha had come from Melbourne and was there for some remedial training. The biggest, blackest, bull-necked and boof-headed Labrador I have ever seen had developed the unfortunate and injurious habit of jumping on people during passive searches of airline passengers. In a smaller dog, it would have been less inexcusable, but with 40 kg behind it, a touch of Alpha's paw was no soft caress.

The burly assistant instructor worked Alpha on a collar instead of a harness, all the better to pull his head back, but the dog persisted in lunging erratically towards the lined-up staff. The arrival of an alpha male in the pack also had the textbook effect on the behaviour of the other males.

Kris, a young and headstrong Labrador with some loveable characteristics, became noticeably agitated at the sight, smell or sound of Alpha, pulling wild-eyed towards his last resting place and frantically scanning the yard for a glimpse of the challenger, barking wildly. It proved to be true that there can only be one alpha male in each pack. Despite his experience, the instructors decided that Alpha still had 'contact issues' when searching people and was to go to another law enforcement agency.

I was to be re-teamed with DD Elise, a Melbourne dog for three and a half years, that had already passed through the hands of two other handlers. Elise was a gold Labrador with 'Bollywood eyes', the dark underlids caused by corrective surgery that appeared to mimic the kohl-rimmed eyes of Indian movie starlets. She seemed to be a high-jumping, happy dog who worked much more steadily than her semi-trained counterparts.

My duties in Tasmania were to involve a lot of work with the police and less of the Customs work at airports. The fact that Tasmania doesn't have any regular international flights created an opportunity for Elise, as she had been passed on from Melbourne due to her lack of enthusiasm for searching lines of airport passengers.

Being re-teamed with an already trained dog meant that rather than try to mould her a little to my handling style, I had to mould to her working style instead. It is more efficient for an old handler to learn new tricks, rather than an old dog.

The real thing

To be re-teamed with Elise, I was moved onto another course with two Northern Territory policemen. The instructor had networked the opportunity of doing some real work with our dogs rather than training exercises, using his contacts with the AFP dog unit.

The Police dog unit Sergeant was a blonde giant in a blue jumpsuit slung with weapons. He was a loud man of football captain-like confidence who ran a stable (kennel) of dogs personally, including two drug dogs and a GP (attack/tracking) dog.

He invited us to attend a warranted premises search in the Canberra suburbs, to be performed at an early hour on a Monday morning to literally catch the suspects napping. The exposure to real search rather than a training set up would accelerate the dogs' training and include all sorts of other realistic aspects like the distracting odours of a druggie house.

Customs have a rather fringe role in relation to the police. We were not really regarded as 'law enforcement' at international airports, and were subject to the powers of $30-per-hour private security staff. Customs was keenly involved in reality-TV opportunities about seizing drugs or weapons, and has hesitantly been going over to an American-style armed service, but the department has its origins in tax collection, and much of that management mentality and culture remain.

The links with policing are largely in the background

— intelligence sharing and surveillance of international movements of cargo, people, mail, ships and aircraft. From time to time other agencies try to take over Customs' functions and Customs bid to take over theirs the usual battle between public service departments for bigger budgets.

The special capabilities of Customs' drug detection dogs put the DDU in the category of necessary specialists to be used by the police, but Customs was never regarded as part of the policing world. Customs dog handlers moved between working for a bureaucracy that relied on facilitation and process and visiting the wild side at the sharp end of house raids with police, one of the most difficult of policing duties.

We waited at the police kennels until the call came and sped through the still sleeping streets to a leafy road of uniformly constructed former government housing, now remodelled to appear like a normal suburb. It was a normal street on a bright morning, with only the occasional jogger or dog walker drifting past. We joined a line of cars parked outside a nondescript residence, its backyard covered in overgrown weeds and semi-stripped car bodies.

A worried neighbour in a dressing gown came over to enquire as to what the problem was. Along the street other curtains flickered as we stood outside, conspicuous because of the barking of dogs in the trailer and two big guys, the NT policemen, in khaki.

The AFP sergeant took one of his dogs in and located bongs, a small amount of cannabis and a smaller amount of heroin between the pages of a book in the lounge. While the owner of the place was being interviewed in the kitchen, we were allowed to quickly take the dogs in to train them on the real thing, not some situation set up by the training centre.

The NT police had most need of experience in house searches. They ran their dogs first, and quickly re-appeared, murmuring encouragement to their dogs who joyously gripped a dummy in their mouths.

I took Elise into a small lounge crowded with furniture and after letting her search a couple of circuits of the room, directed her, at the Instructor's suggestion, to the fireplace grille behind which the heroin-laced book was propped. On the third pass she flicked her head back to the book, at which I encouraged her and the Instructor threw in the dummy to try to make the association with such a small odour and reward.

It was less than a gram of heroin and not an amount that any of the dogs are presented with in training, but all part of the learning process to teach them there's nothing like the real thing.

Recognising a dog's alert and response to a target odour makes the task of the handler appear to be easy, but it is the many shades of grey between a dog recognising a target odour and not recognising it at all, that is really the subtle art of dog handling.

'Reading' a dog is the practice of interpreting small changes in behaviour. Determining the source of the odour requires teamwork, concentration, and quick thinking and reactions from the handler. It is all about knowing your dog – when something unusual happens, directing it or allowing it to lead to give it the best chance of detecting a target odour.

The dog also reads the handler's moods. If the handler doesn't want to work, the dog usually doesn't either. To make my work with Elise a success I had to put aside any reservations and commit to being a team – head and heart!

I was to return to Tasmania to commence duties as Customs officer and drug detector dog handler to the Tasmanian Police shortly, so the faster Elise got used to the real thing, the sooner we would get results in our new home.

On my way

Melbourne receded into the night behind me, a Christmas tree of lights and red and blue bands topping the skyscrapers twinkling as the *Spirit of Tasmania* chugged into a headwind on a wet summer night.

I didn't feel sad to leave as I had never felt that the town had done me much good. I had been away for such long holidays overseas that I had also become a vague 'always somewhere else' or 'planning to go somewhere' person to my friends. The numbing necessities of packing, storing, moving and saying goodbye had so compressed my emotions that I longed for release from such obligations.

Two weeks on dog unit operations as my 'settling in' had reminded me why I had left Melbourne airport and the Melbourne DDU. Most of the Customs dog work is at the air terminal, searching the lines of passengers waiting to enter Australia or clustered around the baggage carousels waiting for their baggage. As one flight arrival blends into the backlog of the last, the queues can literally be endless at busy 'arrival cluster' times, especially first thing in the morning and last thing at night.

The dogs cannot work endlessly and need breaks to get their breath and their focus back every 20–30 minutes. We are much less kind to people, as the officers examining passports on the immigration lines get a break every three hours or so. Having spent time sitting at a computer terminal at which the line of people is constantly added to by the next flight arriving, I could see why airport officers thought the Dog Unit did very little. Most of the time the dog unit is working out of sight or waiting behind the Immigration line for a passenger the dog is interested in.

'The people factory' is a good as any metaphor I've heard to describe the production-line atmosphere of the airport, and I had had enough of it for a lifetime. I had no desire to repeat those experiences, even though I was actually bringing my life full circle by becoming a dog handler again. But in Tasmania, I would be working by myself, and mostly not for Customs. I was more than ready to go south, to the island.

After going through the whole dog training course again, I had cause to reflect on where I was now in relation to where I was when I completed the course as a new handler in 1987. Then, I think I was passed for my energy rather than my competence. In 2004 I was passed for my competence rather than my energy.

At my post-course meeting about my duties in Tasmania, the Detector Dog Training Centre manager looked at me for a few long seconds before speaking. 'Tasmania is an odd place and it takes a particular kind of person to make it work there … but I think we have chosen well,' he concluded.

I could but hope he was right.

CHAPTER 3

SEARCH PATTERNS

Hello Hobart

The floor of the building where Customs was now housed contained about 25 people. Customs used to occupy the grand Victorian sandstone building that is now the museum, with four times as many staff.

My desk was opposite my boss, who was to be my supervisor on non-dog-related matters. He seemed not quite sure what to do with me. I was waiting for my dog, Elise, to arrive from Melbourne, so I walked around, introducing myself to my colleagues and almost as quickly forgetting their names.

I had thought that in the first week I would set up the things I needed most for training Elise – access to drugs, procedures for permissions and operations. I soon learned that nothing gets done quickly, after having four conversations with the officer in charge of security, and three with Admin about the need for a suitable space, a safe, codes and combinations to store the supplies of drugs for training that would be arriving with Elise and the dog Instructor. I was also forced to accept a mobile phone for work and thus was finally dragged kicking screaming into the new millennium, even though I didn't know how to download funky ring tones, text more than a few words at a time or to make smiley faces with punctuation.

The Intelligence liaison officer took me around to the Police and Prisons on liaison visits and I took on the role of a very minor Customs celebrity, meeting the Drug Squad who had, no doubt, felt the lack of a drug dog more than Customs. However, they also looked a bit disappointed to meet me. The previous female handler was a blond bombshell and a frequent attendee at after work drinks and BBQs, if the pictures on the Drug Squad lunchroom wall were anything to go by.

I was to work most closely with the Enforcement team, a group of four officers. The Technical officer and the Intelligence group of four officers also acted in support.

There was one familiar face. I had trained in Canberra in 1987 with a Tasmanian handler and we had been friends ever since. Now it was my turn to be the Tassie handler.

I was housed in the English village locale of Battery Point at the St Ives, a motel with an inconveniently located nightclub attached. The club featured 'doof doof' music four nights a week until the early hours. The music wasn't so bad – the fights in the car park, the roars of pissed boys and the screaming and swearing of their girlfriends were less than ideal.

In a way, I was completing a family circle. My mother had arrived in Hobart in 1958, and lived in Battery Point. She was a 'ten pound Pom' on assisted migration from the UK, and Hobart was her first stop in Australia. It was quite a shock after coming from London – apart from moving from one of the world's capitals to one of its most isolated outposts, she could hardly understand a word anyone said.

I began looking for a share house until I could work out where I would like to live more permanently. Many of the place names in Hobart veer between the twee and the repellent – names like Snug, Sandfly, Eggs and Bacon bay, and Blacksnake plains. Bagdad, just out of Hobart, looked remarkably calm considering the number of car-bombings and suicide attacks I heard mentioned on the news every day.

It didn't take long for me to realise that Hobart is a small town. I started seeing the people I had met during share house interviews everywhere. They were the only faces I knew outside of work. One guy was in the checkout queue at the supermarket and a girl who I had spoken to that afternoon tapped me at the casino. I couldn't remember where I had seen her – she was more formally dressed than a few hours before – and she huffed off, offended.

I bumped into an acquaintance from Melbourne in a Salamanca bar. We were shortly interrupted by a guy with a 'sharpie' haircut. I had seen this guy on the street several times and playing bongos at a folk festival as well. A gifted banjo player who had performed at that festival looked up from the innards of the dishwasher he was repairing in the Customs kitchen. I knew that as soon as I started raiding houses with the Police, I would be bumping into suspects with similar regularity.

Tasmania is the smallest state, with the smallest population and the smallest social circles. My mother had warned me that it took 60 years or three generations before anyone was accepted as Tasmanian. Even children born in Tasmania whose parents came from elsewhere in Australia were still called 'bloody mainlanders'.

The results I could expect from work with Customs, Police and Prisons were likewise likely to be smaller than on the mainland, but I wasn't trying for the big time. I was here in Tasmania trying to find a new life.

Work

My daily task for Customs, which was paying my salary, was to search any international shipping, airfreight or sea freight.

The other Customs section in Hobart, Compliance and Enforcement, sometimes asked me to check freight for them when they were busy. I was looking for items of interest to Customs other than drugs, to see if the description, value or trademarks on shipments were accurate or for weapons or other prohibited items. They needed me not as a dog handler, but as an extra pair of hands and eyes to shift or check boxes. The small number of staff in Tasmania meant that everyone pitched in for tasks like processing cruise ship passengers or unpacking containers.

Although many of the jobs for Elise and I were for agencies other than Customs, I was a Customs officer first and had experience in Customs outside of the Dog Unit, working for many years at the airport and waterfront.

Customs' main work during the Tasmanian summer is centred around the arrival of cruise ships from New Zealand – Australasian cruises between November and March that cater to the well-heeled cruise crowd, mainly elderly Americans.

The cruise ships are a sight to behold, steaming up the Derwent, ablaze with lights in the dawn and sounding long, sonorous blasts on their foghorns to wake the still-sleeping city. The Customs staff are set the unenviable task of processing more than 1400 people as quickly as possible. Long lines of passengers in white shoes and matching white hair file past computers set up in a marquee on the quay side, grumbling and groaning about 'goddamn burracrats' and 'didn't we do this in New Zealand, already?'

My job was relatively simple – to line up the crew and search them with Elise. On cruise ships it isn't usually the passengers that Customs regard as a risk, and as the state has no regular international flights and little international shipping, it was one of the few justifications for having a Customs drug dog in Tasmania.

The spin doctors from central office decided that it would be necessary to counter the bad publicity Customs had been receiving for not having a dog since the previous handler left 10 months before. A little media event was planned to show off Elise and her abilities to the press and TV cameras – a dog performing tricks is always a sure news filler and the cruise boat made a relevant and photogenic background.

I had previously enjoyed my fifteen minutes of fame on TV in the mid-1990s with DD Oscar. Uncle Ben's, the pet food company, were running a series of ads promoting the positive aspects of pet ownership and it was decided that Oscar and I were to represent teamwork. The ads were screened during non-rating periods.

The first time I saw the ad was in strange circumstances – a house set up for Australian Federal Police surveillance. The lights were off and the blinds permanently drawn except for gaps for cameras and binoculars on tripods which were pointed at a heroin dealer's house across the street. A pile of pizza boxes and cardboard coffee cups overflowed from the bin and the TV was left on permanently to disguise the two-way radio noise.

'Hey look, that's you,' said one of the cops, bug-eyed with fatigue, and pointing at Oscar and me on the TV.

A few weeks later I was in a restaurant with my girlfriend. A breathless young lady approached our table and asked, 'Sorry! Are you the guy on ... that dog ad?' My girlfriend glared at her as I bashfully admitted I was, wondering if I could get used to this sort of recognition. Other fans were not so welcome. The girlfriend of a heroin dealer in Melbourne's northern suburbs seemed overjoyed that her house was being raided by someone who had been on TV.

'Oh wow, it's just like on TV!' she gushed. 'It's great to ...' She trailed off as her handcuffed boyfriend shot her a dark look.

'I reckon it's not, for you anyway' I replied.

Oscar received some fan mail from children, and it turned out to be a very long 15 minutes. The ads ran on Melbourne TV, off and on, for four years.

On the Hobart waterfront I set up the demonstration runs so as to guarantee success for the cameras. I positioned a line of parcels, weighting them down with bricks to stop them blowing into the water, and organised a group of officers to line up in plain clothes to display Elise's passive and active responses and search capabilities. Passive response is when a dog sits next to a target odour and active response is when it bites and scratches at a target odour.

All went according to the script. Elise attacked the

cannabis-scented parcel with vigour for the cameras, ripping and tearing the cardboard with enthusiasm. She sat adorably in front of one of the officers attired suitably in shades and a leather bike jacket.

The outgoing Regional Manager did the official announcements about Customs being here to protect our community, and I answered the technical questions, inventing the useful metaphor that until technology became both portable and low maintenance, Elise was our 'machine' to detect drugs.

All were satisfied and I was about to take Elise back to the car when a bearded man with a couple of cameras around his neck puffed up, telling me he was a journalist from the Mercury, the Hobart tabloid newspaper (nicknamed 'the Mockery').

'Is it too late to get pictures and an interview?' he asked. Considering that the Mercury offices are across the road from Customs and a few blocks from the wharf, it was strange that he was the last to arrive, but he may have been covering the paper's next 'scoop' on Princess Mary.

Mary was a Hobart girl who had married a Danish prince, and the Mercury was full of little else. The paper was always eager to lead with a story claiming that Tasmania was more prominent in something than the rest of the country, even if it was because the state had the second-highest unemployment or the highest teenage pregnancy rates. At least with Mary they didn't have to add a positive spin.

I dutifully posed with Elise and answered a few questions while he scribbled. I thought at least I would get a newspaper story to keep for posterity out of it. While I did get a few fluffy seconds at the end of the local TV news, there was nothing in the next day's Mercury, but my story wasn't spiked because of Princess Mary.

The headline was 'Dog attacks sheep', and on page three 'Dog falls off cliff'. Between a story about a bad dog, and a story about a stupid dog, it seemed there was no space for a story about a good dog.

Going inside

Tasmanian Prisons (Corrective Services), like the Tasmanian Police, didn't have any drug dogs when I arrived in 2005 and also relied on arrangements with Customs to provide that capability.

Tasmania had no service dogs of any kind working in its prisons in the modern era, but in the convict days was notorious for them. In the 1800s there was the fearsome 'dog line' at Eaglehawk Neck, a narrow strip of land that separated the Tasman peninsula and the formidable Port Arthur prison. A line of savage dogs chained at intervals, including on wooden platforms over the sea, warned the guards of any escaped convicts trying to sneak past. These dogs were apparently as dangerous to the guards as they were the prisoners.

I had a call from the chief security officer at Risdon prison, inviting me to come down for a talk about operations.

I took the Customs Intelligence and Liaison officer with me as a matter of courtesy and was more than a little surprised when he mentioned that many Tasmanian famalies have had relatives serving a sentence there. I affirmed that I would not mention this to the prison officers, but was quickly learning that social circles in Tasmania are very small indeed.

The security chief and his staff were suitably large-framed and big-moustached men with bear-paw hands. Detaching keys from the jangling clusters on their belts, they took us on a tour of the facility, a 1950s prison that looked more like something from the 1850s, and possibly had its last renovations in the 1970s.

• • •

I had once visited the notorious Pentridge prison in Melbourne (now a housing estate) at the invitation of the Emergency Management Unit that included the dog unit. Their dogs were both drug search and attack trained, and the EMU boys maintained a fearsome reputation amongst the prisoners. They were the trouble-shooters called in to deal with situations that the custodial officers couldn't manage.

The EMU officers gave me a pair of Corrective Services overalls so I would attract less attention, and instructed me not to break a stare when faced by a prisoner. I walked between two officers and noticed when we entered areas, the prisoners' curiosity quickly changed to sullen looks and muttering as they shuffled away from the EMU officers. They knew who handed out the smacks to naughty boys.

Like Risdon, Pentridge was an antiquated place, and the original bluestone made one think of Ned Kelly being hanged. Although this had occurred in the old Melbourne gaol in the city, Pentridge was built not long after that and it showed.

Halfway across an iron walkway on the second floor, we stopped at a cross bridge suspended between the rows of cells.

'This is where they dropped Ronald Ryan' the officer said, tapping the welded-up trapdoor and looking around with evident satisfaction. 'Right down there.' On the ground floor a drain lay directly underneath the trap.

Ronald Ryan was the last man hanged in Victoria in 1955 for shooting a prison officer during an escape attempt at Pentridge. Some believe that the officer was accidentally shot by another prison officer.

We walked on to another corridor of dual iron gates, and then radios on the officers' hips began squawking.

'Shit! Stay here'. They raced to the other end unlocking and locking the gate behind them and pounded off to some trouble, leaving me locked in the corridor.

The prisoners on either side of the iron gates at both ends – one end the inside and the other an exercise yard – gathered and stared through the bars at me, muttering and swearing. I stood, rooted to the spot, staring unblinkingly at them as the minutes ticked past. It might have been ten minutes before the EMUs came back, faces flushed with exertion. The prisoners quickly melted away with the stamp of their feet and I was finally let out of my prison.

• • •

Hobart's Risdon Prison apparently maintained a harsh form of solitary confinement up until the 1980s. Prisoners were let down into a dungeon cell by a ladder, which was then pulled up. They were fed bread and water lowered in a bucket. Shades of our convict past!

From the caged guards' galleries – iron-barred catwalks at ceiling level above each area – we peered into the interior world of Risdon Prison. The trusted prisoners used the workshops and laundries, and the bleak yards were the haunt of those not so trusted. Either way, they were all overlooked by a gun gallery, patrolled by officers armed with assault rifles kept in safes at the end of each gallery.

The inmates, dressed in orange windcheaters and maroon track pants, turned and glared up at as, muttering from the sides of their mouths as we moved past. The place felt not so much like the electronic zoo of modern prisons but the more like the ugly, mouldering confines of the convict era.

Along narrow corridors sheathed in iron bars, the atmosphere noticeably darkened as we entered the maximum-security area through a series of heavy doors and grilles unlocked to let us through and locked again behind us. In a blank concrete box stood a cage where the bad boys walked up and down like junkyard dogs. With nothing else to occupy them, our entry drew instant and complete attention with yelled expletives, curses and the odd question, all ignored. It only took a few seconds for the penny to drop.

'Hey … that's the guy that was on TV!' yelled one of the inmates.

My heart sank.

At once, the prisoner's anger had a focus and the threats and obscenities flew thick. I was shown the cells in there and after a moment we lined up to be let out. One inmate stood at the wire nearest the door, staring up at me on the walkway – only a metre or so above him, but separated by two layers of bars.

'Hey, hey mate, hey mate!' he called.

I was studiously ignoring them all but he persisted. I gathered my impenetrable 'work face' together before turning.

'What?' I barked.

'Do ya feed ya dog Smackos?' he asked, brow wrinkling.

'No.'

'Oh … why not?'

'Doesn't like 'em.' 'Oh.'

The security officers raised their eyebrows.

'Gee, they must like you – you got off easy. Ten seconds on TV and they'll remember you for years.' Great. I was to consider that a form of welcome to my new role across all the law enforcement agencies in Tasmania.

I was called back to Risdon Prison for a three-day operation involving Elise, searching staff and visitors over a long weekend. I have rarely had a dog-handling job I enjoyed less.

The security section officers trust few except themselves, as corrupt staff are believed to be the means by which large amounts of drugs and contraband get into the prison. Visitors allowed contact visits with prisoners with good behaviour privileges are known to conceal balloons containing drugs in their mouths and pass them over during the expected passionate kisses.

The environment was ugly and hostile, lots of searches were required, and my expectations of finding any drugs were low. A small quantity of drugs – we are talking of a gram or two – kept in someone's mouth for a short time is likely to leave little odour for Elise to find. I did my best to try to read any small changes in behaviour during her search, and to her great credit, Elise worked with commendable application. She nosed close to the line-ups of staff without jumping on them and ignored the potential distractions of the lunches in their bags.

She did show a close interest to several of the nursing staff and in particular the pockets of their vests where they usually keep medication. Attraction to this chemical odour at least affirmed that she was searching closely.

Our real problem came when the searches of visitors began on the Saturday afternoon. Families and friends of the prisoners have to apply for a half-hour time slot for a contact visit.

After being screened by metal detectors, groups of maybe 30 visitors are led through the outer door of the prison and into the vehicle port.

Once they were all in the port, the security manager informed them that they must agree to be searched by the dog if they wished to enter and that any person interfering with the dog or being found with contraband would have their visit terminated.

Anyone opting out at that stage was free to leave, but would then be picked up and searched by the Police Drug Squad waiting in the car park.

The officers had been briefed to watch for any sign of someone swallowing or attempting to dispose of any drug balloons they had in their mouths.

On the first run, there was one small boy with his mother amongst the ranks of adults and Elise refused to go anywhere near him, baulking hard away in a slinking, frightened fashion, despite my attempting to encourage her to pivot back and search him. Perplexed, I initially put this down to some individual factor of the child giving off signs he was afraid of dogs, but soon found on the next line-up that Elise was afraid of children.

Whole families were present – except for dad who was inside – and Elise swerved away from them.

I had never seen a working dog exhibit this type of behaviour before – none of the training exercises I had done with Elise involved children. She had done only a few airport immigration lines in Melbourne where a dog can be expected to miss searching the odd person in lines containing hundreds of people.

I had not been given any indication by Elise's previous handler or the training centre that she had a problem with children, and this was the wrong time to find out with so many eyes on us.

Worse, it seemed she was alerting, standing on her hind legs and swinging quickly as if following a drug odour, but completely refusing to go near the families despite my reassurances, directions and encouragement. It was embarrassing and I could see the quizzical looks on the faces of the security officers.

I collected my thoughts and reined her in to a short lead to concentrate on doing extra search passes up and down in an effort to get a consistent indication of a drug odour. As much as I didn't like the thought, I knew that it could be that a drug odour was coming from a child and she was scared of that child. Her fear could only be the result of mistreatment when she was a puppy.

I was unable to get any more specific indication as to which person was likely to be the source of her alert and admitted to security that I was unlikely to get her to search at all around children. I shortly heard one of the officers telling another, 'The bloody dog is scared of kids.'

In spite of this inauspicious beginning, Elise and I still had much time to serve in Risdon.

CHAPTER 4

DIRECTING LOW AND HIGH

True north

I made a trip 'up north' to Launceston at the request of the Drug Squad to search some passengers at the airport. They had received a tip-off that a young man would be taking a large quantity of cannabis on a flight to Sydney. The police didn't know when he would check in and their powers to search without warrant were limited to the public area before check in.

Quarantine dogs regularly search passengers arriving from the mainland to uphold Tasmania's strict quarantine regulations which protect the state from pests and diseases. I wore a plain khaki t-shirt with my blue fatigue pants, guessing that if I didn't say otherwise, the passengers would assume that Elise was a Quarantine dog looking for fruit and was part of the normal airport inspection.

The cops in plain clothes sat on the seats nearby waiting for me to point out anyone I wanted them to search, while I directed Elise to sniff each passenger approaching the check in. It involved an hour and a half of slow work, passengers arriving in ones and twos, inside the hot terminal – the aircon was off to 'save power'.

I spied a guy that fitted the description given and Elise searched him without change in demeanour. The police then approached and also searched him but to no avail – another false lead.

We also had an appointment for a ship search in Bell Bay, a port about 30 km north of Launceston. The Iranian bulk carrier was carrying a compliment of 24 crew and eight family members.

• • •

In Melbourne in the 80s, the venerable DD Oscar had made our only seizure of any note on a ship search – another Iranian vessel berthed in Geelong. This was during the bad old days of the Iran–Iraq war when Iranian vessels were found to be harbouring stowaways fleeing from military service, and crew members jumped ship to avoid the great slaughter occurring in their homeland. To control such activities, Iranian and Iraqi vessels also carried 'political officers' on board to watch the activities of the crew. It's like the old cold war joke. Why do Bulgarian policeman travel in threes? One knows how to read and write, another knows how to use the telephone and the third keeps an eye on the other two dangerous intellectuals.

The penalty for being caught deserting or assisting others

was no joke – being placed under arrest until return to the homeland and then a short stint clearing mines with their feet. The political officers wielded great power over the crews and even the captain, and hence weren't used to taking orders from anyone, particularly Customs officers.

The leader of the search team, an old-school Customs officer with a walrus moustache and bald head, informed the nervous captain that the search team required all areas to be unlocked. The dog would not enter the prayer room, which would be searched manually, and all crew would be allowed to take their prayer mats and Koran from their cabins before the dog entered, as long as they could be searched in turn.

The political officer pulled rank and ordered the crew to lock their doors, telephoning the Iranian consul in Canberra to make the search a diplomatic incident. Perhaps he was in on the hash deal. The search halted while frantic negotiations took place in Geelong, Melbourne and Canberra.

The final decision was to leave it up to the search team leader. Taking a sledgehammer, he yelled, 'Stand back!'

While two Customs officers held the political officer back the hammer swung against the political officer's cabin door, the contact booming down the corridor. When that lock was broken open all the others magically opened without need for the hammer.

The search itself was fairly inconclusive except for bottles of whisky and pornographic magazines being found in the ceiling of one room. The dogs did alert to a number of storage bins around the engine room that no longer contained any drugs.

With time ticking away and an exhausted search crew waiting

for the order to depart, I took Oscar on one more pass of the deck area. On the rear deck he swung hard and attacked a large coil of rope stacked beside the winches. It concealed a plastic-wrapped package the size of a thick paperback which contained about half a kilo of hash. It appeared that the previous dog reactions and the intelligence had been correct, and our target had been stealthily moved around ahead of the search teams. There were still another four and a half kilos somewhere, but further searching failed to locate the stash.

• • •

At Bell Bay, the Captain greeted us with a glimmer of gold teeth and the offer to make 'special coffee'. He observed that people here, even the fishermen he had seen entering the mouth of the Tamar, looked happy,

'Not like in my country' he lamented.

The crew were mustered and obligingly lined up along the narrow corridor surrounding the Captain's office. Elise sniffed them as they stood still, occasionally rising up on her hind legs to search higher up, chasing some mysterious scent or lack of personal hygiene. She didn't pay any particular interest to the crew and we then worked on through locker rooms, storerooms and offices in the ship, and the cabin of anyone unlucky enough to be near.

It seemed from their cabins that most of the crew preferred to sleep on the floor and they hurriedly rolled up their sleeping mats before the dog entered. Dogs, to those of the Moslem faith, are dirty animals, but I did not take Elise into the prayer room or allow her to touch their Koran or prayer mats.

Despite the hot weather, Elise worked well, the first time

I had worked on an operational ship with her. Normally ship searches are conducted by two dogs, working in a tag system, one resting while the other worked, as ship searches are long, difficult and the interiors of ships are hot because of the engines below. I didn't have the luxury of another team to help. Elise was stepping up to do the work of two dogs.

Well hidden

The premises search on the corner house at Glenorchy in Hobart was unremarkable by local standards. An average suburban house, neither neat nor terribly messy, with two excited barking dogs, a child having a bath and a couple of bags of dope in the kitchen. The police had been told the couple were speed dealers, but couldn't find any evidence for amphetamines.

I closed off the kitchen with its cannabis smell and made sure the dogs were secured in the backyard, hustling Elise straight down to the three bedrooms at the rear. An officer from the Hobart Drug Squad was assigned to assist me.

In the first she was very interested in some rolls of leather under a bed, deep sniffing at the hide in a perplexed manner. In the main bedroom she attacked a drawer, in which a few traces of cannabis were found in a box. In the spare room I called the assisting police officer in as Elise began frantically twisting back and forth in search of the scent, wagging her tail.

'She's on to it – just watch'. Elise went up high, jumping against badly balanced boxes and tins up on shelves that came crashing down. I pushed aside the fallen items-books, tools and broken appliances, and made way for her to search.

She propped on her hind legs at a workbench that carried

a sewing machine and inhaled deeply along its heavy base, attacking the metal with her paws. The staccato rhythm of her claws was loud in the room. I threw her dummy against the machine and she neatly snapped it up, growling and grunting with deep satisfaction as I shook the other end that protruded from her teeth.

The policeman examined the machine for a few seconds and then pushed it back to reveal that the machine swung back on a hinge from the base, the cavity underneath holding a zip lock bag with half an ounce of cannabis.

'Well' he smirked, 'Looks like Elise has got the case all stitched up'.

My relationship with the Hobart Drug Squad was going through a second honeymoon period. On three jobs in a row Elise located drugs that were unlikely to have been found by conventional means. When the Drug Squad rang me for a job in Bridgewater that week, my first question when I heard the name of that depressed suburb was, 'Is it worthwhile?'

Bridgewater is on the far side of what the police called 'the flannelette curtain', the area north of Creek road that occupied most of the Police resources in Hobart. Real estate agents smoothly referred to 'the Border'.

'Yeah, it's a joint that we have turned over three times and never really found anything, and the guy is always boasting that he has it hidden so well. There's a lot of activity around the house – cars pulling up there all the time – so we reckon we will need the dog to help us on this one.'

The police were inside already and judging by the swept hardwood floor and corner shelf of photos, the owners were considerably more houseproud than many of their neighbours.

Elise moved through the three front bedrooms quickly. In the corridor, she picked her head up and darted through the lounge and into the kitchen, swinging wildly in front of the sink. I pulled open the cupboard door and it came away in my hand, Elise lunged at a shelf holding the usual cleaning products, pulling away with a can of drain cleaner in her mouth. I took it and threw it into the sink, praising her lavishly. Elise lunged again as I turned her towards the kitchen cupboards nosing the bottom of the fridge and scratching rapidly against the white enamel.

I chucked the dummy toy out of my pocket and she leapt away bearing it and me towards the door.

'Just those two areas!' I called over my shoulder to the police.

Elise flung herself on her back on the front lawn and kicked her legs wildly with joy.

Back inside, the suspect slumped over the kitchen table while the police retrieved some ounce bags of grass, a set of scales and a page of notes from under the fridge. 'Just personal use stuff' he insisted.

'So what are the scales and this list for?' they asked. The paper was covered in calculations involving amounts in grams, numbers of bags, sums of cash and people's names.

'Dunno, just junk'.

'I don't think the magistrate's going to see it that way'.

I turned my attention to the sink. I picked up the can of drain cleaner and saw that the metal pop top was unopened, shaking it as my suspicion grew. I turned it upside down and tried the base, twisting each way. It unscrewed in a counter-clockwise direction and came away to reveal 14 zip lock bags of grass.

Dog beats man again.

Two steps forward

Dog training never takes just one direction as there are many different circumstances in which a Customs dog must work. It is not a matter of just teaching a dog the odours that it is expected to find and then expecting it to adapt to every environment it will search in. A dog usually performs differently in each scenario according to the training it has had. Ships, planes, bags, boxes, houses, letters, cars, fields, people, and all the variations of each scenario must be replicated in training for a dog to work efficiently.

A dog may search a line of suitcases in an airport well, but not a line of parcels in a mail centre. As the dog improves in one area, it may get worse in another. The process of dog training is constant and always involves taking two steps forward and one back.

Dogs are like children – sometimes they surprise and sometimes they disappoint. Elise, like almost all other drug dogs, would sometimes perform unexpectedly well on a difficult training run and then be a baffling failure on an easier run.

When a run goes badly, it means that hours of planning and preparation have been wasted. More hours will be needed to set up and perform several exercises to bring the dog up to the expected level. It starts with a more basic presentation of the target odour and scenario, made progressively more difficult in terms of the amounts and types of drugs involved and in the presentation, length and complexity of the runs.

Training is the constant background occupation of dog handling. The work performed may vary, but training is constant and never regarded as complete. A dog by nature operates on instinct – but it also thinks. About 80 per cent of dog behaviour is innate but 20 per cent is learned. Dogs are constantly re-interpreting human actions or trying to circumvent them to get to what they want – if they can get away with it.

It only takes a couple of repetitions of an action for it to become a part of a dog's learned behaviour. They notice quickly the cues given by their handlers – their moods, tone of voice – lots of our unconscious movements or habits are giveaways to a dog.

A handler's task is to plan training which will encourage improved performance, and to create a constantly updated list of troubleshooting exercises to change habits and behaviour that have already been learned.

There are always some elements of randomness in a dog's actions when some part of its innate behaviour takes over from the learned. We humans have to take responsibility for most of their problem behaviours.

• • •

Up until the late 90s, Customs used simulated drugs to train their dogs rather than the real product. 'Pseudo' was a neutral powder base saturated in acids emitting the strongest odours found in heroin and cocaine. It was much easier to use than real narcotics because it was a benign product with no narcotic properties and therefore was administratively much easier to handle in terms of the department not having to be concerned about its loss or theft.

However, using 'pseudo' and working under the methods approved by the Canberra training centre seemed not to be bringing much success. Many experienced handlers were telling Canberra that although their dog could find the 'pseudo', it had failed to identify real heroin or cocaine. I removed Oscar from all pseudo training and only reinforced him on runs on Police and Customs seizures – only real drugs.

I saw an opportunity to catch the imported drugs the second time they were moved – when the drugs were being transported interstate. Surely the level of precautions and concealment were likely to be lower, making things easier for the dogs. I went to work on a personal project to assist the Australian Federal Police and Vicpol at Melbourne airport. We could get Customs dog access to domestic flight luggage by working under police powers. The police were all in favour, but the most difficult thing to do was to convince Customs that this was worthy and necessary.

Presenting my domestic screening project to Customs, I said, 'I am going to tell you a story, and after you have heard it, I want you to think whether you are still against my domestic project'.

I told them the story of a German entomologist in the Costa Rican jungle who was sure that there was more life in the jungle canopy than met the eye, but was unable to prove it by conventional means of collection. He laid out plastic sheets on the ground over a hectare, and fired a pesticide mortar bomb up into the canopy. Within minutes, hundreds of species that had never been seen by man before were collected on the sheets below.

There was silence for a few seconds when I finished the tale. I got the go-ahead!

The project was successful in interdicting drugs being transported interstate, resulting in several major investigations and in giving the dogs training on real drugs. Oscar's proficiency at locating drugs in domestic luggage became so refined I could often tell what they were and where they were stashed in the bag from his reaction.

One evening, he took a close interest in a sports bag. In an inside pocket was a matchbox containing a couple of capsules packed in cottonwool.

The sweating passenger swore that the pills were migraine medications and he begged to keep them. The police let him go but held onto the pills, finding out a few weeks later after forensic analysis that the capsules contained Australia's second-only seizure of a new designer drug called 'Nexus'. Oscar earned a place in the national intelligence summaries for that.

The following year, after a few more failures to detect drug shipments, and much determined lobbying by handlers, Canberra finally relented. Pseudo was banished and real powder drugs were finally issued for training. Detection of powder drugs by dogs increased immediately.

In the finest public service tradition, this change was implemented by Canberra as if it was their idea – no recognition that the handlers who had called for this change for years had been right all along.

• • •

The homegrown variety

It was imperative to get Elise identifying the Hobart varieties of amphetamines quickly. I needed to build her abilities and the confidence of the police in us.

The Drug Squad Sergeant offered me some paper that

had been wrapped around a seizure of local amphetamines to use in training Elise. I appreciated his interest as we had only imported ice – crystal methyl-amphetamine – to train on, a substance which smelt different from the local types of powdered speed cooked in farm labs by Tasmania's bike gangs.

In the early stage of my relationship with the police, getting their confidence in Elise's ability was a key element in keeping them happy and myself in work. However, if she didn't recognise the smell of the speed wrapping at all then that could pull the carpet from under us and bring about a lack of police confidence in her. One slip might mean being less likely to get the good jobs – high-stakes searches of premises where quantities of drugs had been cleverly concealed.

Elise was not performing well identifying Customs' stocks of crystal meth so far – perhaps the local variety of amphetamines (or 'go-ey' in local slang) didn't smell anything like what she had been trained on. We borrowed a vehicle thought to be clean of drug odour and tucked the rolled-up paper bag into one of the seat pockets.

Elise searched the front seats of the car without any interest. When we entered the rear, I was just about to lean in and direct her to search some specific locations when she banged her nose down on the seat pocket as if magnetised to it and began scratching strongly. I threw the dummy in with lavish praise and pats.

The Drug Squad Sergeant seemed impressed and I was somewhat surprised at the strength of her identification. I couldn't say what smell she was actually finding, but it must have been close to one of the drugs she had trained on. Shame she couldn't talk!

She had put one paw firmly forward for the position of Tasmanian sniffer dog.

Neanderthal and the black snake

The Drug Squad had lined up two premises searches – one in Hobart in the morning and another in Geeveston the same afternoon, a one-hour drive along the south coast.

The target in town was a guy known to them as 'Neanderthal', a speed dealer in the notorious low-income suburb of Bridgewater. He was apparently so named because he resembled our hairy forebears.

Neanderthal had been raided several times previously and now took precautions. He had a strong security door and a CCTV camera to warn him of visitors. The entry plan involved two officers rapidly levering open the security door while another two wielded a battering ram against the door. Hopefully he wouldn't be watching his CCTV as they approached, or the drugs would be down the toilet by the time the police got inside.

My job was to search, not to crash doors or heads, so I was to sit around the corner and wait for the call that told me the house was secured. Someone knew and hated Neanderthal enough to provide detailed information on where and how he hid his drugs, mostly between packets of meat in the freezer.

Our little motorcade rolled into the street behind the house at 9 am and I sat with the window down, listening for the hollow boom of the door going in. I heard nothing but a few minutes later one of the jeans and t-shirt clad officers waved me in. I parked out front, going in first without Elise to safety check the area for any doggie dangers such as used needles or unrestrained pets. The front door and its security screen were intact.

'Did he open it for you? I asked.

The officer pointed to the line of hotted-up Fords in the driveway, parked bumper to bumper through an open driveway gate into an unsecured backyard.

'No, we just sneaked down the other side of the cars and found the back door open'. A small chink in Neanderthal's armour.

The suspect sat inside in his pyjamas, moodily smoking a ciggie while his missus and little girl did their best to sound like it was the start of a normal day. They were waking up to their lives being out of control, again.

I hate seeing children in these circumstances and always wonder how the parents explain all the police suddenly being in the house to them.

Outside, the street was busy with mothers pushing prams and children gathering at a bus stop for school. The really worrying thing was that no one paid any attention to the men carrying Glocks and a battering ram or myself in uniform with Elise. A neighbour pulled in on his motorbike and did not pause as he went inside. It seemed that there were a lot of similar small businesses and frequent unexpected closures in Bridgewater.

The locals complained about what a bad suburb it was, but it was a 20-minute drive from the centre of Hobart, with water views and green fields all around. The houses looked basic but neat, from the outside anyway. They should have seen the bad outer suburbs of Melbourne or Sydney.

The afternoon job was part of an ongoing Geeveston murder inquiry, exposing the dark underbelly of a seemingly quiet orchard and timber town. Investigations, arrests, informants and listening devices were exposing a web of crime, violence, drugs, theft and complicity.

A motorcycle gang owned many properties in the area, using them to cook speed, grow marijuana, store firearms and stolen goods and, apparently, breed prize goats.

I followed a line of unmarked police cars, bouncing along a rough track until we reached a heavy steel forestry gate. The police smashed the lock and led me to a two storey stone farmhouse, surrounded by sheds filled with junk and a paddock of 50 expectant goats. No one was home and after some waiting to see if the 'principal' or person named on the warrant would appear, the lead detective decided to search the exterior areas before deciding on entry to the locked house.

The CIB were leading this operation. One of them was fashionably attired in an all-black outfit and he had clipped a shiny plastic sheriff's badge to the pocket of his black shirt to complete the image.

The information specified that drugs and guns might be hidden in the sheds and I did my best to encourage Elise to search around the drums of chemicals and rolls of rusty wire, despite some intimidation from the herd of unhappy goats and some aggressively territorial chooks flapping at us. Some cannabis was found in a paint tin in a back part of a shed we couldn't access due to the piles of fence posts and wire. I intensified our efforts around the perimeters, looking for the amphetamine stash.

Elise searched all the likely markers of posts, rocks and planks scattered around the clearing without success so the search widened into the surrounding bushland. A chicken-wired corral of large marijuana plants was found, and several other sites that appeared to have been recently emptied of dope. Small groups of officers spread out, overturning pieces of wood, rocks and old oil drums in their quest to find the hidden speed stash.

A piercing scream pierced the afternoon quiet followed by two of the female officers stumbling out of the bush. A tall blonde officer dashed onto the road. She was in a frenzy, stuttering and shivering in terror. She was closely followed by another officer in a similar state. They had turned over a piece of roofing iron and disturbed the rest of a large snake, which had reared up.

The sheriff-badged detective presented himself as a snake expert.

'Are you sure you weren't bitten? You might not know … but I have heard that after a while, if you feel your arm or leg going numb, it is already too late!' he suggested.

She tore off her jacket and pulled up the legs of her pants as if they were burning, searching for the fatal wound.

'I could have been bitten … did it bite me? Maybe it did! I think my arm's going numb, oh my God!' she wailed.

Before he could suggest that she should continue undressing and he would volunteer to suck the poison out, the detective was pushed to the back. Other officers told her that being bitten felt like being hit with a cricket bat.

The officer sat shivering in the car, surrounded by her grinning workmates. She turned to her partner. 'Why didn't you shoot it? I would have had my gun straight out if the snake had been having a go at you!' she declared.

In the bush, as well as in town, it's the quick or the dead.

CHAPTER 5

THE HANDLER IS A DOG'S GREATEST LIMITATION

Elise in ecstasy

Customs often search by means other than physically opening packages and unpacking every item. The mobile x-ray machine is a great labour-saving device used to identify boxes that need to be looked at closely because the image is inconsistent or the material too dense.

Likewise, using a detector dog for searching cargo is a broad screening tool to direct any physical search to the items indicated by the dog. Cargo searches are mostly hard work for both officers and dogs.

Either way, shipping containers need to be unpacked manually at some point to either run the packages through the x-ray or run the dog past them or both. If they are too big to go through the x-ray they have to be laid out so Elise has the best access for sniffing. It all involves a lot of heavy lifting and carrying at some stage of the examination process, no matter what mechanical devices are available.

Most of the larger cargo examinations in Tasmania occurred at the Customs shed at Bell Bay north of Launceston, where all available officers from north and south were needed for the long and tiring task of unpacking, examining and repacking.

The conditions in the draughty, dusty shed were rather primitive compared to those on the mainland, and for a long time almost all the moving of boxes was essentially done by hand rather than with forklifts – very, and potentially injuriously, old school.

On the grounds that the container potentially held drugs – that, after all was what they wanted Elise to check for – I declined to assist with the unpacking to avoid contaminating myself with drug odour.

The hard-working team laid the boxes out in as many rows as would fit in the shed, and I ran Elise back and forth over and around them. She occasionally showed some interest in a few (as distinct from responding to them) and these were sidelined for a full search. Otherwise, the boxes were then fed back into the container via the x-ray machine as a belt and braces approach to doing our very best. In keeping with the cooperative spirit, I usually helped with the repacking if there were no dog jobs that I had to rush off to.

I don't think there was ever a drug cache discovered in cargo in Tasmania, but undeclared weapons were detected by use of the x-ray on a number of occasions.

Items too big to go through the x-ray, like cars and furniture, were examined by Elise or an officer. The use of the Ionscan and other trace analysis machines was also another useful form of technology which could help define what needed human intervention.

The upgrading of technology is always presented as a constant threat to the old-fashioned method of using detection dogs, and machines are often marketed as a competing technology rather than a complimentary one.

The first lesson to be learned is that all methods have their limitations. Everyone is aware that dogs have limitations but it is rarely ever mentioned that every other form of technology has its limitations too.

I have mentioned a few. X-ray machines are not able to penetrate or distinguish all materials, and anyone who travels on aircraft knows how inattentive the airport baggage security operators are. The electronic explosive trace detection devices we have now become used to being wanded down with are all compact versions of gas chromatographs. These machines are all either over- or under-sensitive, as every law enforcement agency knows, and their other great limitation is that they can only spot test, not track target odours like a dog.

Detection equipment can be a great support in circumstances where dogs are not the most useful tool, and dogs can be great detection tools where the machines cannot go. They are complementary, but I know who I would rather have as a workmate.

The express mail

The Drug Squad, with a little prompting from me, decided that it might be worthwhile searching the Easter mail arriving from the mainland. The extended holiday often meant extended trading hours for Hobart's drug dealers, requiring extra supplies to be sent in.

The catch was that with express mail – a cheap and timely way to send drugs and anything else through the post – an early start was needed. The guaranteed next-day service meant it arrived early in the morning before being delivered that day. Mail screening is a short but intensive task, as we had to work within Australia Post's tight timeframes to identify individual articles of interest to the police, and let the others go for delivery.

It was a triple screening arrangement, involving the police, Elise and me and the Customs x-ray van. The express mailbags were opened and their contents tipped into wire cages by the postal staff and then passed on to the police. Bleary eyed and in much need of coffee at 6 am, they first removed any commercial mail and items they regarded as low risk to go straight through to the posties.

The bulk of the parcels were passed on to me to set out in lines for Elise to search and then run through the Customs mobile x- ray machine. It is a complimentary system involving human intuition, canine physiology and radiation technology. Elise might not find some small amounts of drugs or drugs that she is not trained to find, which is where the x-ray machine came in.

On the first morning Elise had not alerted to a parcel containing a small number of heavily packaged ecstasy pills that showed up on the x-ray screen like smarties dotting a birthday cake. However, the x-ray cannot distinguish cannabis from packaging clearly, something which Elise managed with ease.

Sometimes the outward appearance of a package, bearing an unlikely name or a lack of return address, suggested further investigation, even if the x-ray or Elise didn't provide any clues. A few of these contained all sorts of religious and cult newsletters, paraphernalia, miracle charms, curses or blessings. There was a willing market for this stuff in Tasmania, a state known for its born-again Christians and isolated communes.

The Customs Tech officer showed me a letter that had originated in the UK, forwarded by one of the big mail centres on the mainland. The address and the forwarding note said it all about the mainlanders' view of the island state.

It was addressed to, 'Sheriff and the Bumpkins, the country, Australia'. The mail sorter in Melbourne or Sydney had scrawled 'try Tassie' underneath.

During my previous service with the Melbourne Customs Dog unit, I helped Customs officers at the Melbourne mail centre to assess letters screened out in an effort to see what my dog was not detecting. Any letters we thought suspicious were put into a pile and then double checked by another. On one occasion, my fingers picked up a smooth border of a flexible card and then a slightly expanded area in the centre. It could have been an embossed greeting card but the raised area didn't seem to follow any decorative pattern. When opened, it was a plain birthday card that had been spilt open and the edges re-glued with 1000 tickets of LSD inside.

LSD is odourless so a dog wouldn't detect it on its own. The paper of the tickets is also too thin for x-ray machines to detect and depending on how well sealed it is, there may be few trace elements to be detected. This leaves the detection down to human intuition, and we all know the variability and limitations of that! Sometimes it works.

Nothing is perfect when it comes to such detections, and everything has its limitations – people, dogs and machines.

The Hobart Drug Squad showed me the first lot of ecstasy pills the x-ray indicated, half a dozen dark green, brittle tablets bearing a Mitsubishi logo, visible on the screen as a line of tell-tale dots along the side of a CD cover. I had the pink and white varieties of ecstasy from European laboratories only to train on, and each had a distinctively sweet smell – different from the Asian variety. However, I accepted Elise's limitations with a heavy heart and congratulated the x-ray operators on their find, hoping we would improve the next day.

On the first run the next morning, the start was promising as Elise swung onto and pawed at a letter with such vehemence that I flicked it away to stop her from tearing it open. The strength of the reaction made me suspect it contained cannabis and one sniff confirmed it. Two runs of lines of parcels later, she swung onto one package, pausing to put her nose on a bulge in its profile and inhaled deeply, then worked on.

I waited with interest to see the x-ray image, as she had acted much differently from the little nods of the head that I associated with a less than definite dog reaction, called a 'change in behaviour'. A conglomerate of bubbly shapes in the dark shadows of thick paper appeared on the screen, and the police massaged the satchel open using a hairdryer to unstick the adhesive flap. Out tumbled two plastic bags of green tablets with Mercedes logos.

'Elise. Yes!' I cried, punching the air with relief.

The Drug Squad called their operations centre, who readied the look-alike postal truck for a 'special delivery' to the addressee by police acting as posties.

It's a case of, 'Package for you, mate. Sign here, and don't pull away too quickly or the cuffs will cut your wrist.'

This was our first powder drug hit, and under the eyes of the Drug Squad, upon whose confidence I depended for much of my work.

The highs of summer

Tassie has natural beauty, and drugs to spare.

I was enjoying the change of pace and scenery in Hobart, free of the traffic problems that I disliked so much about Melbourne and the car-choked and endlessly dreary suburbs.

The light was constantly changing on Mt Wellington and I savoured the view of the Derwent River and the green mountain several times a day on my trips between the city and the airport. I really believe that Hobart and Cape Town have got it over every other city in the world for visual grandeur.

I found a look out point on Rosny hill on the east side of the river to take pictures of the mountain in sun, cloud and snow, a small homage to my new home. Summer never gets as hot as on the mainland, and in the rest of Australia they had been having a scorcher – high 30s to 40s for weeks on end, accompanied by bushfires. Hobart only reached temperatures in the thirties on one hot Sunday and I joyously revelled in the first real day of the season and took Elise to the beach.

She wasn't one for swimming, just running into the water up to her abdomen and waiting anxiously as I swam.

Summer is really the busiest time in Tasmania.

The Sydney to Hobart and Melbourne to Hobart yacht races begin filling Constitution dock with all manner of sleek craft and the town visibly bulges with the post-Christmas influx. The Taste of Tasmania festival adds to the bulge with all manner of food and drink available along Princes Wharf, and MONA has attracted a large following. And of course there was the Falls Festival – Tasmania's rock concert that shares its name with a rock festival in Lorne, Victoria.

Summer is also the busiest time for Customs in Tasmania with the arrival of cruise boats from New Zealand. They have many more people on them than cargo ships – usually 500 passengers and 300 crew members – and a lot more space.

The passengers were mostly aged Americans and presented little drug risk as far Customs was concerned so most of my efforts with Elise were for display. We selected an area of crew cabins and facilities to search if no direct information was available to narrow down the target.

Police sniffer dogs had been used at big music festivals on the mainland to signify that the police were doing something about drugs, mostly in response to the usual overdoses of ecstasy and related public outcry. There was also much outcry over the use of dogs as harassment of the wrong end of the drug trade.

The Greens in Victoria had begun a 'Sniff Off' campaign to have sniffer dogs removed from public venues, and this was quickly followed by a stunt from the political satire group 'The Chaser'. A reporter loaded up his pants with fresh meat to attract the dogs outside the Melbourne Big Day Out.

The Hobart Drug Squad had requested the presence of Elise and the Customs x-ray van at the gates of the Falls Festival, feeling it would send a strong message. Customs management didn't agree and thought that such an overt presence at such a well-attended event would be difficult to defend. As police work was such a prominent part of my duties, a compromise was reached. I could screen passengers at the airports as part of police operations to target people arriving for the festival. This would do something to assist in the screening process, give us some much-needed airport work and, hopefully, a few hits to improve Elise's enthusiasm for searching passengers, the lack of which had been the reason she had been sent to Tasmania.

I also had to refuse a request by the Launceston Drug Squad to work the ticket queues at the 'Day on the Green' and other concerts, but told them we could work the airport arrivals instead.

In Melbourne, I had busted several of the band managers, performers and technicians for the Big Day Out festivals as part of my domestic airline project with Vicpol in the 1990's. DD Oscar had 'rolled' one of the well-known Australian impresarios of rock and roll twice, as well as band managers carrying portable pharmacies for the performers.

The Launceston Drug Squad hadn't seen a dog searching a line of passengers before and sent two plainclothes officers to blend into the crowd, watching for any of the usual suspects they wanted Elise to sniff and for my signal to intercept a target.

Just before the flight landed, one of the officers was called off to another job in town but he arranged a replacement – two very fresh-faced uniformed constables. I began to give them a quick explanation of how Elise works and what I wanted them to do when suddenly the flight was down and quickly disgorging passengers. 'Watch me!' was all I could offer to try and make sure that we didn't let any hits slip away.

The terminal at Launceston was essentially still a country airport. Before air security rules were implemented to exclude the public from the tarmac and other areas, it was possible to wander down to a low cyclone fence next to the planes and greet people before they went upstairs to collect baggage. Bags were collected straight from the trolleys in a shed to the side, a jumble of people pushing and dragging bags in all directions.

I had a garden area before the steps to the arrivals area to work in, standing near a Quarantine officer unenthusiastically asking passengers if they had any food and telling the public to stay out of the walkway.

Elise was straining at the lead to go but I waited until the first passenger had got to the end of the walkway to give her the longest continuous line of search. On the 'Find it!' command she bowled along into the oncoming legs, while I called loudly to passengers to keep to their left as they went past the dog, watching her and quickly dropping and re-catching the lead as she scooted between people, causing cries of alarm.

Passengers were used to the Quarantine dog standing in one spot as they walked past, not a dog in amongst them.

'New dog, is it?' I heard asked several times.

'Yep. Just keep to the left.' Getting to the steps, the passengers on several flights began to bank up along the walkway, making our job a bit less hectic as they were only shuffling forward.

Elise suddenly swung back towards the tarmac and bolted along the line. I let go of the lead and scrambled to regain it as she swung back again and chased an odour into the milling passengers in the garden. 'Excuse me. Stop! Dog coming through,' I called, my head down while trying to read where the target odour was coming from.

She switched back and forth behind a guy in sunnies, curiously searching the ground instead of the people. I put a hand on his shoulder to stop him and Elise dived down, lying on her stomach and began pawing at his hi-top basketball shoes.

'Good girl!' I praised her and looked up for my police back up. The two uniformed police were over in a second and took the guy aside to talk with him.

'Shoes!' I specified, in case they hadn't seen Elise's reaction. I thought of working on through the dwindling numbers and then bringing her back to reward her, particularly as she had such an unusual and persistent reaction. Before I could direct her back down the walkway she darted around me, whipping the lead around my legs and pulling hard into the passengers at the steps. She sat behind a man pushing forward into the crowd at the steps.

'Stop there, thanks!' I called as I jumped between people to catch up to Elise. He half turned, showing an eye bright with fear and pushed forward up the steps. 'Hey. Stop!' I called, struggling to get Elise through with me.

As he reached the top an anonymous figure in sunglasses shot out an arm. 'Police!' he cried as the man crashed, face first, into an open police badge wallet. Elise skidded into a sit beside him and I slammed the dummy down at her feet. 'Good girl'.

'In a hurry mate?' asked the officer.

Playing tug of war with Elise, I looked up to see the uniformed police escorting the 'shoe man' through the doors.

'Nothing there,' said the young constable. 'But he's wanted on some warrants so we'll take him in anyway.'

'You did check his shoes?' I asked, rather surprised and disappointed at no result from such an unusual reaction.

'Yeah, he said it might be traces from the floor,' he explained.

The 'runner' had been carrying cannabis and pills and had been going to the concert to share or rather, sell, the love. The uniforms left with the two men in the back of the van.

Half an hour later we got a call from the watch house sergeant.

'Your dog hit a guy's shoes? Yeah, well that dog could teach these kids a thing or two because when my guys searched him properly, there was about half an ounce of cannabis between the insoles! It's not all bad mate. They owe you an apology and they owe us a slab!'

This was a step towards building a profile for Elise and me in Tasmania and extending our efforts to the airports that otherwise had little police coverage.

That afternoon a car had been intercepted speeding south to Hobart. The fellow was in such a hurry that he overtook an unmarked police car at about 150 km/h. In his bag were a variety of pills he had intended to sell at the concert, but had been warned off by his mates in Launceston that the Police had a drug dog searching people going to the concert. Bad news travels fast and we had obviously had an effect even in the places we weren't searching.

It had been a good day for some, especially Elise. With those positive finds and rewards at Launceston, I knew she would be raring to come back to the airport.

CHAPTER 6

CHANGE IN BEHAVIOUR

Total recall

Elise and I received a welcome direction to travel to Sydney for post-course recall training at Sydney Airport (SAP), and a ship-search training course, specially designed for the DDU. The course sounded both practical and fun, and also took us out of Tasmania's winter for a few weeks to Sydney's relative warmth.

A few months after the end of each dog-training course, a 'recall' training is planned. Its purpose is to determine how dogs and handlers have developed after operating in the real world and whether the handler is able to troubleshoot and regulate the dogs' training. A few exercises were set up to test the dog's proficiency on different batches of drugs, but recall training doesn't have the overtly critical nature of the initial training course in Canberra. It is more about guidance than admonishment.

Recall training was at the busiest airport in Australia – Sydney, the big smoke. The officers at SAP asked me what it was like working in Hobart.

'Well, you have an airport here, at least,' I replied.

The dog unit kennels in Sydney are unique – a split-level building with the kennels set like dungeons under the offices. The exercise yards seem to be oddly shaped, shoehorned around the edges of a car park and auxiliary buildings. The unit is in a light industrial strip bordering a residential area. The surrounding residents constantly complain about the barking of dogs echoing from the basement.

Due to the lack of space Elise was put in one of the 'isolation' kennels, a glass-walled enclosure used to stop sickness spreading to other dogs. It was a dim humidicrib from which she was (unsurprisingly) grateful to be released each morning.

Sydney is the Australian city with the largest population and welcomes the greatest number of international flights, so there are a correspondingly high number of drug seizures.

• • •

For Elise and me it made quite a change to get a shot at a big drug seizure on an international flight. In Hobart, we had no international flights and certainly no contact with people coming directly from high- risk regions such as South America.

The 'Bali Nine' were caught in Indonesia at a time when many Australians were caught attempting to traffick drugs, notably in countries where the penalty for such offences is death. It was a hot topic of conversation in Australia.

Shapelle Corby's blue eyes and rabbit-in-the-headlights look had burned deeply into the Australian psyche and the debate over her guilt raged, with most people tending to believe in her innocence. For a few months, it became an inescapable topic of conversation, especially if it became known that you worked near an airport, had anything to do with drug law enforcement or had a second cousin who had been to Bali.

I wish I had recorded my opinions the first time I had to give them on one weekend trip to Melbourne to save my energy the next twenty times I was asked.

I worked in a special Customs Tarmac unit that concentrated solely upon airport and airline staff and aircraft, and any internal conspiracies involving them. I searched planes and flight and ground staff whilst looking to uncover the kind of conspiracy that many people believed took Shapelle Corby to jail in Bali.

In the year I was there, we didn't find any major syndicates but we were working our way up the information chain, starting with people stealing from duty free and airline stores and pressuring them to give up information on more serious matters. We were also appealing to the honest staff to assist us, and slowly gaining their confidence by being impartial, discreet and reliable.

Our efforts were bolstered by the invaluable presence of an AFP liaison officer who within an hour could get the sort of information that it might take us weeks to get from Customs intelligence, if at all.

The sort of criminal activities that have been reported – baggage handlers inserting and taking things from baggage

– do occur. I just don't know if that was a factor in the Corby case. There are not too many pieces of luggage with the spare space to hold a 4.1 kg bag of marijuana like the one Shapelle had in her bag, but then again, if you work in either Sydney or Gold Coast airports, you are assured of seeing more than a few surfboards transported per day.

One of my workmates from Melbourne airport was asked his opinion on the Corby case by a girl he had just met at a party. His opinion that she was probably guilty was met with disbelief, tears, then anger and several blows aimed at his head. Her friends intervened as they dragged her away.

However, there was no ambiguity about the guilt of the Bali Nine – having drugs strapped to your person is irrefutable evidence.

• • •

The ship search training course on Sydney harbour included the necessary theoretical sessions about the construction of ships, yachts, and detailed the hiding spots of contraband seized in recent years. The week was possibly the most fun I had had in the department.

A large part of the practical instruction on the safe boarding of ships included 'height management' – ascending, descending and abseiling with the dogs. The mysteries of the masses of webbing, buckles, straps, clips, ropes and devices that we had brought with us from search kits, were revealed. The mixed group of handlers from NSW, QLD and myself learned the nautical arts of tying figure eights, double loops, the intricacies of the Alpine butterfly, the uses of the 'Gigri' descender and the A3 ascender and how tight one really needed to have the groin straps done up on a harness to avoid lasting damage in a fall. We learned ascending and descending ladders and tunnels towers and bridges, and to trust in the knots we had tied.

And the dogs needed to trust us.

A new type of support harness had been developed, in which the dogs could be suspended from an attached sling, lowered and raised on ropes and carried, if necessary, like a bag. The poor dogs wore confused expressions as they were strapped into their elaborate harness, and then gave the forlorn looks of the condemned as they were clipped onto lines and swung out over the edge of a drop, their tails firmly between their legs.

We had to hold their front and rear legs together until they were clear of the edge, as they would naturally scramble to touch any projection and could easily catch and break their limbs as they descended or ascended. Once suspended in the air, they were cheerfully encouraged by their handler to see it as another part of their job. Search and reward exercises were commenced immediately after being unclipped, to let the dog know that it was all part of the grand game. The dogs were not as frantic on being hauled from the ground up, as the slow rise seemed less threatening than being pushed off a building.

Once all these skills were tested, the highlight of the week was the practical search exercise, practicing boarding and searching ships from Customs boats. We screamed across magnificent Sydney harbour in twin-engine Zodiacs, all geared up in life jackets, helmets and climbing harnesses, the dogs in their flouro safety harnesses and yellow 'Muttluk' boots to protect their paws.

The Marine Group pilots zoomed us under the Harbour

Bridge, past the Opera House and around into a bay where the rusting hulk of the ship the 'Cape Don' lay, long under arrest for non-payment of port charges. A rope ladder was lowered from the deck perhaps 30 metres above our heads and one by one we clipped on and scaled the flaking metal, then fixed a rope and pulley to a stanchion and hauled the dogs up from the zodiac.

Once on board, we performed the opposite procedure, lowering ourselves and the dogs down into the dark, musty smelling holds to perform a search, then hauling the dogs up to the deck and climbing up after them. Various amounts of drugs had been secreted in the cabins, engine room workshops and passageways, so it was a positive exercise to fix in the dog's mind that all the strange equipment and procedures still equalled a search and find game with a tug of war toy as the reward.

The Marine Group took us the long way around Sydney Harbour on the way back to the training centre. We tore out through the Heads at Manly, the little boat nosing down the troughs of the Pacific Ocean. When we returned to Tasmania I managed to get the Police to organise a sea boarding exercise to help Elise and me keep in practice. After many phone calls and weeks of negotiations, I secured the assistance of a police launch to take us down the river to a fishing vessel found in a prohibited zone of the Southern Ocean.

I went up over the side on a rope ladder and lowered a rope for Elise to be clipped onto. Once she got over the shock of leaving the deck, she seemed quite happy swinging in the harness, her tail wagging. We were fully prepared and a happy team.

Green buds over the white cliffs of Dover

The Drug Squad requested Elise's services for a job. They couldn't tell me anything about it other than it was on the south coast and we were looking for cannabis. We arranged to meet at the Huonville Police Station at 10 am.

There is a beautiful road that winds along the banks of the Derwent to the south coast. Fishing boats cluster in the bays, moored off weatherboard villages, and stands of forest fence in the cow paddocks. The area is very attractive, but as I worked my way through the south coast towns with the police, I was beginning to regard these scenic spots as dens of iniquity. I was reluctant to visit on my weekend trips.

The rendezvous is never in the town in which the raid is conducted, as the sight of a convoy of cars pulling into the local police station sends the bush telegraph rattling. In those neighbourhoods people will be flushing their green and staying away from home for hours.

The information was that a cannabis crop had been harvested and was ready for sale, the usual Tasmanian produce story, but in this case the informant had reason to believe that some other people also knew this and were planning to impersonate the police and raid the house. The preparation included hiring a white sedan, purchasing a blank search warrant for $1000 from an un-named source and packing guns in case the crop owners didn't believe the charade. The police had to act fast, not only to take down the crop owners, but to protect them as well.

The two target houses were on the same road near the town of Dover and owned by father and son. I assumed that the son was the grower and dealer, and the father, in his early 60s was an unknowing accomplice.

I tagged along behind the unmarked police 4WD going to the father's house, drawing up in the drive of a neat, fussily decorated residence with a well-kept garden and little dogs yapping a welcome.

The police, dressed in casual clothes, stepped out to be greeted by a dinkum farmer-looking bloke, silver haired, a rosy, outdoor complexion creased by the sun and wind. He carried an expectant look on his face as if about to chat with some misguided tourists.

'G'day'

'G'day'

'Yeh'. He had the sing-song voice of the countryman.

'We're the police.'

'Oh yes,' he replied cheerfully, apparently not knowing what the visit could be about.

'We've got a search warrant for you.'

'Oh yes?'

'It's for drugs. Do you have any drugs in the house?'

A slight pause. 'Oh ... yes,' he said cheerfully, as if describing a prize pumpkin.

'Where are they?'

'Oh ... inside. Come on in.'

I could smell the rich, spicy odour of fresh cannabis as I reached the front door.

'There's a bit there isn't there?' said one of the detectives with some surprise.

'Oh well ... my son's wife smokes a bit.'

I looked over their shoulders into the room where three large styrofoam fruit boxes sat on the floor brimming with fat green buds the size of cocktail frankfurts. There were about six or seven kilos, and the whole house stunk of grass.

'Now she'd have to smoke a lot to make a dent in that,' said the cop with the disappointed air of a schoolmaster.

'Well yes, I suppose so,' replied the owner sadly.

There wasn't much Elise and I could do in the place except give her an interesting training exercise by letting her run around from the front door into the huge cone of cannabis smell. After looking rather dazed she eventually dipped her paw into one of the fruit boxes rather uncertainly and scratched some of the grass out. I tossed her dummy in and took her down the road to the son's place, a larger and more utilitarian house but no less respectable.

Often the houses of people in the drug trade look like arrows pointing to their disreputable activities, but not in this case. I couldn't have picked either the old man or his son out of a line up, but I could smell cannabis as soon as I stepped out of the car and the cops pointed me to the door at the side of the double garage. The grass was inches deep on the floor, with drying stalks hanging from the roof.

There wasn't much I could do here either, and so I went into the house where the police were preparing the son and his heavy smoker wife for a formal interview.

'Oh sorry, the place is a bit of a mess,' fussed the woman, more conscious of the opinions of unknown visitors than the effect of 10 kg of grass in the shed.

It struck me as a slice of Tassie life. It was a reminder that the growers and the dealers often came from very different backgrounds and that cannabis was really just another form of crop.

You know when your dad gets old and you both have to

make an effort to do stuff together. A lot of guys go fishing together, or build a barbeque, or sail model boats.

In Tassie, togetherness seems to involve growing monster buds.

Ships and chips

Hobart was home to most of the summer cruise ship visits, Antarctic and Southern Ocean research vessels but imports to and exports from the state mostly happened elsewhere in Tasmania. Although Hobart liked to call itself the state capital, it was not the centre of everything.

Customs also had staff in the northern port of Burnie, a smaller port on Bass Strait with a more direct line to Melbourne. As well as being Tasmania's largest general cargo port, Burnie hosted the occasional cruise ship visit during summer – its proximity to the beauty of Cradle Mountain is the drawcard.

Stepping out of my role as dog handler and into my role as Customs officer, I assisted the other Customs staff in processing the passports of the hundreds of passengers aboard the international cruise vessels of the Holland America line – the MV Vollendam and the MV Statendam.

● ● ●

Burnie puts on an outstanding welcome for the passengers. A children's choir sings on the docks, musicians play and the Mayor in his gold-chained regalia greets the passengers and poses for pictures. In spite of all the hoopla visitors are probably a bit disappointed when they leave the dock. Burnie is a very industrial country town and not really the type of place for tourists. It is dominated by a huge pile of woodchips awaiting export (the short tour of the state's forests, as I refer to them) and it does not have the visual appeal of Hobart, with its sandstone buildings beneath a green mountain.

There is also something about the look that men in Burnie seem to adopt – all curled lips, shaven heads, flannel and tattoos accompanied by a certain stiff-legged strut that suggested the prison yard.

Most of the passengers board buses waiting at the dock to whisk them away to Cradle Mountain, but the occasional passengers opt to look around Burnie for the day instead. I would try to get them to reconsider.

'One of the most beautiful natural areas in the world is just a bus ride away. That's what you've come to Tasmania to see isn't it?' I'd ask them.

A couple of hours later on, I would see the same passengers wandering in the town centre, looking bewildered and vaguely annoyed, having already exhausted the tourist highlights of Burnie.

• • •

There were no woodchip piles in Hobart because the main woodchip mill and loading facility was out on the east coast at Triabunna, about an hour and a half drive along a narrow, winding road.

The timber company Gunns ran the woodchip mills and associated ports for southern and northern Tasmania at Triabunna and Bell Bay respectively. The logging trucks from the southern forests headed for the Triabunna woodchip mill right through the centre of Hobart. The enormous size of many of the logs served as a reminder of how old the trees were.

The influence of Gunns, the taxpayer-subsidised cutting of forests (called either harvesting or destruction, depending on your philosophy), and the business of exporting huge volumes of raw wood were at the heart of a great political, social and economic divide in Tasmania. Protestors from environmental groups were involved in an often bitter struggle to stop Gunns with demonstrations, blockades and lobbying, often sitting on log tripods blocking roads and chaining themselves to forestry equipment, including the chip mill at Triabunna. The response from the forestry workers was often fury and violence. Tasmania was a national symbol of the 'Greenie versus Redneck' divide.

The woodchips were exported to China, Malaysia and Japan via direct line bulk carrier ships that docked at Triabunna with their holds empty and departed full. It was the task of Customs to board these ships and check the foreign crew, passports and paperwork.

Triabunna was another place for Elise and me to search the ships and crew as a standard Customs task but getting onto the ships was far from straightforward.

The Customs boarding team and I followed an escort vehicle down a winding, truck-rutted mud track sticky with brown wood pulp, through the log and chip piles and onto the wharf.

The wood chip loader towered above the dock like a box-girder brachiosaurus stretching between the mill where the logs were chewed up into chips and the ship. A conveyor belt poured the loose chips down into the open holds. The dinosaur's tail was on the ground and its head hovered over the ship.

The dust and woodchips shaken off the belt showered down continuously underneath the loader where we parked, necessitating wearing helmets, goggles and dust masks. Unfortunately for Elise, I had none of this equipment for dogs and could only take a water bottle to wash out her eyes, nose and mouth.

Entry onto the ship was also via the loader as the wharf was mostly too low to use a normal gangway. I looked up at the catwalk steps zigzagging up about 50 metres. I put Elise into her harness and put on my own climbing harness, clipping her to me with slings and carabiners so she was securely attached and I could have both hands free to hang on. I am not good with heights and watching out for Elise as I guided her up and up the open metal grid steps was a good way of keeping my mind focussed and away from the ever-increasing drop beneath us.

The last part of the catwalk was alongside the conveyor on the long neck, the woodchips pinging and clattering down through the grates. I tried to keep Elise moving forward, as the strange circumstances and my own apprehension were causing her to try to turn back. With a hand firmly under her harness and crooning praise and encouragement we walked on.

A short ladder dropped down to the deck as the loader belt continued onto the hold. One of the boarding officers slid down ahead of me and reached up to hold Elise as I swung her off the edge on the climbing sling, keeping the momentum going before she could hesitate. I praised her lavishly and marched her around the other side of the accommodation block for a drink, to wash her face and a rest. I was panting and shaking.

'Jesus, I hope we don't have to do this too often,' I muttered to Elise. I knew that climbing down would be worse than going up.

'Crew are lined up and ready!' called the boarding officer.

I didn't feel ready but fortunately Elise did, and sprang up, pulling me through the door.

'Find it!' I called belatedly, letting go of the lead as I stumbled into the corridor. I caught up with her at the end of the line up, the Filipino crew whistling and chuckling with delight at the dog. Elise searched avidly low and high without incident and pulled away down the corridor for the next place to search.

Boarding ships with a dog at Triabunna was one of those situations only encountered in Tasmania and required developing a particular set of skills, but Elise was more up to it than I was, especially when the chips were down.

Elise finds the needle in the haystack

The phone rang while driving back from a rather unpleasant search of a container of sacks of fishmeal at Bell bay, but it had been no doubt more unpleasant for Elise's elevated olfactory senses than mine. I was rather deflated to hear the Prison security manager on the line.

'What's your availability next week mate? We've got an urgent job.'

'Well, if it's urgent I'm available.'

'Information is from the manager of the farm (the prison

farm – minimum security) that a big package of drugs is somewhere there and we've got to hit it early next week.' My heart always sank when I received requests from the prison.

I didn't relish the combination of the gloomy and threatening atmosphere, the large areas and numbers of people to search with the expectation of only finding a small amount of contraband, if we were lucky. A big package for them was a small one for Customs or Police.

A Customs technical officer came along to assist me and we followed a mini-van filled with hefty prison security officers to the prison farm.

This was my first time there. The place had a reputation because of the regularity of escapes during the summer. On average one prisoner fled every two weeks, many of them only weeks short of completing their sentences. When prisoners escape in Tasmania, they never leave the state and are always picked up within a couple of weeks, found with their mothers, girlfriends or at a mate's house – often an ex-con.

The farm is only a prison in the sense that there are custodial officers there and the inmates are locked in after hours. They're fairly free to roam the farm on their duties during the day. A couple of years ago the police discovered that two farm inmates in for burglary had been slipping out during the night to do more jobs. They were back by morning duties with a perfect alibi. It is also pretty easy for drugs and any other contraband to be smuggled in. They could be left near or passed over any of the boundaries, and on into the main jail at Risdon via the prisoners sent back there on day work.

A group of about 20 men were lounging around the buildings. These, I realised with some alarm, were the prisoners, the sort of group contact that would have meant trouble in Risdon.

There were also five officers only to supervise 90 prisoners, odds that I wasn't keen on if something got started. But there was a very different atmosphere to Risdon.

There was some conjecture about our presence, but not the shouted obscenities and curses of the main jail. One guy was swearing continually in the background, but it didn't seem to be directed at us in particular.

The Governor briefed us. A prisoner informant he trusted had told him about a mixed package of drugs that was hidden on the farm and was due to be moved to the main prison by the work detail. I don't know what they reward their informants with, but I assume it must be worth the risk.

The areas for search mentioned were one cellblock, a row of farm sheds and the milking shed area. I had hoped that it wouldn't include many cells, as they closely resemble ship's cabins, and Elise had already searched too many of them without reward.

It was a big job for one dog and a needle in the haystack challenge considering the area of the farm we were being asked to cover.

The officers made sure the prisoners were kept away as I was led down to the 'Toorak' block and set Elise off on a long run of cells and amenities rooms. I did my best to keep Elise's and my own spirits up by changing the intonation of my voice and switching to working her off lead to encourage her to feel free to show some independence.

She loved jumping, and once in a cell she would jump onto the bed and then take a bold leap across the desk – great for searching the shelves above but not so good for the prisoner's prized possessions on the desks. I grabbed several models made of matchsticks and ink drawings to avoid having a paw planted irreparably upon them. One house-proud crim had placed a tablecloth over the desk, which almost sent Elise flying off the other side as she slid along it. Unfortunately his legal papers and toiletries slid straight into the adjacent toilet bowl.

After a break to let Elise sniff around the rose garden, we moved on to the tractor sheds. There was a farm dog, which had been removed from sight for our visit, but the smell of him was everywhere, as well as other animals like cats and chickens, and all caused distraction to Elise in her drug search. Much of the time I thought I could see that she was actually enjoying the interesting animal smells with little thought of looking for drugs.

After these sheds, the officers suggested I also search the gym and woodwork shops, as I feared they would. Now I was here, I suspected they might try to have the complete farm search operation on the cheap, by getting Elise and me to do it all – time for a serious chat with the Security Chief.

'I can't do the whole place, as much as I think you'd like me to. You've got to narrow it down or we are going to run out of steam soon' I pressed.

'OK, lets go up to the milk sheds then,' he conceded.

It was the usual farm arrangement, a shed with corrals and milk pumps, another full of stainless holding tanks and a lot of stockades, everything wet with disinfectant wash down.

There didn't seem to be too many spots to hide something other than a tearoom and some storerooms, which were pretty Spartan.

The real potential lay in the hay shed – a two-storey corrugated iron roof under which lay a stack of about a thousand bales about 40 m long and 6 m high. If I had been hiding something, it would definitely be in there.

I walked around the hay shed, clearing obstacles like loose wires, rusty nails and the odd stray cow grabbing some hay on the sly. At least it was a different sort of area from those we had just done and Elise seemed to enjoy the change.

We commenced the search, Elise straining at the lead and cutting a circuit around the outside of the stack, her enthusiasm in sharp contrast to her lack of enthusiasm in the cells. Elise jumped up on the stepped front of the haystack and immediately changed behaviour, putting her nose down to the straw and sniffing feverishly. She stopped at a join between bales, and after inhaling deeply, pawed at it a couple of times.

'Good girl, that's a good girl!' I praised her, a little breathless.

The prison officers ran over.

There was a little empty hollow made between the bales that may have held drugs. I was certain we were getting close and moved down the side of the stack to where the officers had piled up some hay bales as steps to reach the top of the stack.

Elise nimbly ran up to the top and I puffed and stumbled after, falling over on the top with a cry of 'Find it!' to keep her moving while I recovered. She ran from side to side, swinging rapidly and stopping at several depressions in the lines of bales. I directed her to search some obviously disturbed areas, but she was drawn on as if by some invisible magnet. She swerved towards the rear of the stack where the bales met the corrugated iron wall. She kept her nose down and suddenly stopped about half way along, pawing at a crack between the bales.

I praised her and pulled her back and removed the top bale. I released her and she sprang down into the gap, digging furiously at the hay. I again pulled her back and praised her as the Tech officer pulled at the stalks.

'I can't see anything there,' he explained.

I let Elise go and she plunged her nose down into the bale, emerging with a plastic bottle between her teeth.

'Oh!' I cried in surprise, and knocked the bottle out of her mouth. As she lunged for it, I tore the dummy from my pocket and tossed it on top of the bottle.

'Good girl!'

It's called blind subbing and is done only when you are confident that the dog is onto one of the target odours, but it's really a gamble calculated on one's knowledge of the dog.

The Tech officer opened the top of the bottle and I glimpsed a sheaf of plastic zip locks containing, pills, powder and green.

'That's it! Good girl!' I crooned, jubilant.

The cannabis in it certainly helped to increase the odour and I was as proud as punch of my dog. Elise had found the needle in the haystack, albeit not one of the hypodermic kind.

CHAPTER 7

METHODS OF
CONCEALMENT

Value adding

I had not had much to do in the northern ports of Burnie and Devonport since my initial visit after arriving in Tasmania.

Despite the trips to Bell Bay and Launceston every few weeks, the concept that I would receive adequate notice of any shipping jobs and be able to alert other agencies and ports to 'value add' to the trip only worked in theory. In practice, an accurate predication of a ship's arrival time at Bell bay could only be made a few hours beforehand and I was often expected back in Hobart that day.

I decided to take a different tack and encourage requests by the Devonport Drug Squad by suggesting I could be there on such a date if they had any jobs going. I thought it would provide a change – a couple of days away, a change of scenery, and a few more hits to our credit.

Dog-friendly accommodation in Devonport was difficult to find apart from four-star B&Bs. Staying out of a kennel and in a normal room for the night was always a bit strange for Elise, having been born and bred a working dog. She lived in the kennel and the car and only went into houses to search them.

I let her investigate our accommodation. She looked at me occasionally, wondering when the 'Find it!' command would be given. She sat and watched me intently for directions until I laid her sleeping blanket down at my feet and positioned her on it – a sort of 'I order you to relax' command.

After half an hour of watching me watch TV, she let go a deep sigh of confusion and put her head down between her paws. Before I went to bed, I would put her blanket down on the bathroom floor next to her water bowl and shut her in.

There was some expectation from the office staff that I would keep the dog in the car overnight, as that is what previous handlers had done, but I refused. The dog spent enough time cooped up in there during the day, and if I couldn't see her she was out of my care and control. Fortunately, Elise was also a very quiet dog who rarely barked, although I would hear the occasional groan while she was sleeping or the sound of her dragging her blanket around.

The Devonport Drug Squad were an enthusiastic group. They had lined up three houses to search that morning.

The first was a minor speed dealer, a woman with a young child who flogged go-ey amidst the piles of unwashed clothes and a décor which featured badly made Native American ornaments and dolphin statuettes.

The information was that she kept the go-ey concealed in a beer can in the fridge. She was slow to answer the door until our knocking was followed two heavy blows of a sledgehammer. The beer can was empty, but Elise responded to a wallet beneath the cushions of the couch that contained a wad of $50 bills, and a mat on the toilet floor.

Perhaps we were a bit too slow to get in – it seemed most of the drugs had been exchanged for money and the rest flushed during the 'sorry, I didn't hear the knock' delay.

The owner of the second house in east Devonport won high marks for neatness but lost points due to lack of intelligence.

Known as a local grower, he watched me point out a tin of cannabis seeds that Elise had located in the back of a chair. He was rather proud of his ability to grow cannabis.

'Take a good look, mate, a real good look. Ya don't see 'em like that, do ya? Na, they're top stuff mate, I grow the best,' he proudly exclaimed.

'I guess so, but you're just about to lose them,' I reminded him.

Elise had also indicated up high in the lounge, and behind the stereo speakers on the mantle. I found a tin containing some of the grower's prized heads. 'Where was that?' he demanded.

'Ahhhh, now ya taking stuff off me I'd even forgotten I had!'

The third house was an ordinary suburban home that had been brought to the attention of the police by a door knock around their area seeking information on recent car thefts. A detective asking the couple if they could help with information on crime in the area was sure that he could smell cannabis strongly from the front door and had trouble keeping a straight face.

He wasn't mistaken.

The bearded bloke who came to the door looked deflated when told the reason for our visit, and stayed silent until the sergeant pointed to me and told him a search dog was coming in.

'Oh all right, I'll show it to you,' he sighed.

There was an ounce in the lounge cabinet and six, six-foot high plants in a hydro set up behind the garage. They didn't really need Elise, but could, in future, just put the detective on a lead.

The Spirit of Tasmania

The State opposition party were loudly repeating their claim that the ferries from the mainland were carrying 'carloads of drugs driven straight into our community' and that Taspol had failed to check this obvious barn-door like entrance port.

I was called into the Customs Regional Manager's office to respond to a Canberra enquiry about the number of times I had been asked to assist Taspol to search vehicles or passengers from the Spirit.

I hadn't been asked to and didn't think my predecessor had either.

The Government had responded to the Opposition criticism with a statement that Taspol had performed five drug searches on vehicles this year, assisted by Customs dogs. It was a political answer to a political question. The formulaic statement about combatting 'drugs in our community' concluded with a call for a police drug dog to be stationed at Devonport. Despite a good and cost-free relationship with

Customs, Taspol were now making enquiries about getting their own dogs, one in the north and one in the south, despite the lack of requests I had received from them.

This political push for Taspol to have their own dog unit after 30 years using Customs dogs created a growing uneasiness about my position in Tasmania. If they did get their own dogs, I would have little to do in the state except the routine Customs work – a few low-risk freight runs and ship searches – I certainly wouldn't make any drug seizures.

Prisons were scheduled to get their own drug dog from Customs the next year, and I expected to lose most of my requests from Prisons and a few Taspol jobs to them as well. From being the only dog on the island, the place could become overcrowded in a year's time.

The level of debate about the 'drug ferry' was about as sophisticated as that over Shapelle Corby. What the government didn't bother to consider when replying to the opposition was that the sort of drugs they were talking about – amphetamines and ecstasy pills – didn't arrive by the car load, but in much smaller quantities in mail and the bags of air passengers, and no one seemed to be asking how often the parcels or passengers were checked at the airport.

Carloads of drugs do *leave* the state via the ferry. The scenario was not discussed in the island state, but drugs from Tasmania are shipped to Melbourne by the carload.

I had searched the *Spirit of Tasmania* going the other way (to Melbourne) a few times, as part of the Melbourne dog unit in the 90s with the Victoria Police. The summer marijuana crops were packed into the backs of vans and taken for a voyage to a more lucrative market on the mainland.

Bigger than Ben Hur

The name of the ship was written in red on the arrivals board, the sign that it was due for some special attention from Customs. The Iranian ship was more special than I first thought because Tasmania didn't receive many ships arriving directly from overseas and any vessel that made Tasmania its first port of call was given a higher risk rating than it would have at the busier mainland ports.

My supervisor called me aside and informed me in hushed tones that a crew member of the target vessel was a possible match for a terrorism suspect. This would be more than an ordinary ship search.

Having worked on immigration processing at Melbourne airport I knew that people with Arabic names came up as possible matches for a similarly-named terrorist on a daily basis – any similarity in birth dates would have the Immigration officers staring hard at the passport and the details on the screen.

The impending arrival had our office working feverishly on reports and operational orders – this notable level of activity was a sign that Customs central office in Canberra and other government agencies were taking a close interest in the case. An Australian Government security agency were going to send two officers down to check out the crew's identity and with the marshalling of the Feds and greater Customs resources, the operation was becoming a big thing for Tasmania.

I had been suffering from a cold, despite having been given a flu vaccination a few weeks before, and with a dripping nose and heavy limbs decided to take my first sick day in six months. It turned out to be not a restful time. First of all, I couldn't get in touch with our cheerful and devoted kennel hand, who looked after the dogs in our absence, so I had to go in to the kennels to get Elise out for some exercise, clean her kennel and return in the afternoon for a repeat to feed her. In the afternoon, the phone calls began from Hobart, Canberra and Sydney.

As this was a CT (counter-terrorism) search, and not targeted at drugs, this meant bringing in one of the Customs FEDD (firearms and explosive detector dogs) as the primary search tool. The Melbourne FEDD handler was in Canberra helping out on a FEDD training course, and the next available team was in Sydney. After several calls back and forth, it was agreed that the handler and his FEDD Oprah, a black Labrador, would fly down from the harbour city and stay overnight in Hobart in case the ship's arrival was delayed.

The female staff of the Customs dog-breeding centre in Melbourne chose the names for the pups and those names reflected their love of daytime TV.

I set up a kennel for Oprah, but there was some administrative argument as to who was to pay for the handler's hotel, a matter not apparently included in the bottomless budget that the magic words 'counter-terrorism' conjure.

• • •

Several hundred thousand dollars had been expended two years previously on sending two Australian Customs dog teams to the US to undertake special FBI training on detecting chemical weapons precursors.

This sounds impressive and certainly ticked off some counter-terrorism checklist in the high offices of government, but after the dogs were released from Quarantine two months after the handlers returned to Australia, it became clear that no one knew what to do with these special teams. The obvious thing was for them to search suspect imports, aircraft and vessels for terrorists and their ugly weapons, but apparently no one had thought of what to do if a Chem. dog alerted or showed a change in behaviour while working. As the substances they were trained to detect were potentially weapons of mass destruction, searching for, identifying and securing those weapons required special skills, training and the assistance of any number of experts – military, transport, science and police for a start.

A dog may show a change in behaviour (CIB) during any routine search – a turn of the head, a wag of the tail, extra interest in sniffing a spot – that may indicate an item worth examining.

Or perhaps just another smell that they are interested in!

The dog is an imperfect machine and may not be absolutely sure as to whether the smell they are getting is one they have been trained on. The odour may a be a little different due to minor chemical formula changes or it may be heavily concealed so that it is not enough for the dog to decide whether to respond or ignore it.

A good handler follows up all CIBs. The difficult seizures are made by closely watching the dog and working together. If a Chem. dog shows a CIB, then rather than the officer checking out the item and moving on, the area would have to be shut down, cordoned off and specialist assessment and search teams brought in. Transfer these procedures to an airport or port and you can begin to understand the hold ups and expense involved.

Consequently, the Chem. dog teams were told to stay out of 'all operational areas' until further notice and spent their days practising their expensively-acquired skills doing exercises in deserted buildings.

• • •

I had the luxury of playing second fiddle on the ship search assisting Oprah and her handler rather than doing it all myself. The suspect party on board was the Chief Engineer, which didn't narrow down the search at all – the whole ship was his work area and needed to be searched.

I greeted the Sydney FEDD team at Hobart airport and showed them our kennels and a quick tour of Hobart before attending Customs House for a briefing. I was able to arrange for some seized firearms and ammunition to be hidden around the office to give Oprah a test run and to motivate her after the flight.

Initially, the search of the target ship ran as usual, with a muster and documentary check of all crew. Iranian vessels are a little different to most cargo ships in that many of the officers' wives and children are aboard. They are listed as supernumeraries or catering staff to meet regulations but are required to attend crew checks.

The line-up that presented itself for the passive search by Oprah was more like a family gathering, with the men lined up along the mess room walls and the women in their headscarves and bright clothes sitting with the children in the lounge. The men laughed as the women shrieked and shrank from Oprah and the children laughed in delight and strained to pat her. Oprah didn't show any particular interest in the crew, so a couple of them were selected at random to cover the fact that the Chief Engineer's cabin was being searched, and to attempt to make it appear as if all the attention was a routine check.

On unlocking their cabins, the crew slipped off their thongs and groaned in dismay as the dog's paws and our combat boots walked over their none too clean carpets. Oprah showed a small amount of interest in a spot in the chief's cabin as he watched impassively from the doorway. He was a large man, bald headed and from Kazakhstan, not Iran.

Forget your conceptions about Islamic terrorists. His connection was thought to be with the Chechens, not Al Qaida. As we worked through the engine control and storerooms, a call came over the PA for the chief that two men from the 'Maritime Safety Board' were waiting to see him. He left in an unmarked car for a chat with the spooks from a security agency.

I got Elise out of the car for a run in the engine room, a hot, noisy and difficult place to search. Her nose in the air, she gamely leapt from a pile of crates to the top of some storage racks, tracing the source of some elusive odour. I set the search team the task of following the overhead air conditioning ducts, in case the smell that interested Elise was coming from elsewhere. Elise's CIB was inconclusive, as most of them are, but as a handler your job is to follow any lead the dog gives you. Luckily they hadn't brought the Chem. dog on board – it would have created a difficult situation.

On being returned to the ship, the Chief Engineer lamented that he would now have the difficult task of explaining to the

Iranian authorities why he was taken away from the ship.

The interview with the chief was apparently as inconclusive as the search, but the gloomy mantle of counter terrorism had settled to stay, even in sleepy Tasmania.

Sandy Bay

The Hobart suburb of Sandy Bay is one of the city's more expensive areas, the home to many of the established families and old and newer mansions.

It is also home to the Wrest Point Casino and the University of Tasmania's main campus and associated student houses. The uni has a road and faculty buildings named after T T Flynn, the rather less famous biologist father of flamboyant Tasmanian turned Hollywood actor, Errol Flynn. There is surprisingly little named after the internationally famous star in Tasmania, just a small park at the end of a beach not far from the university.

The Wrest Point Casino sticks out like a sore thumb into the Derwent River. It was Australia's first (legal) casino in the early 1970s and looks like it. When I was living at Parliament Street someone thought it a good idea to string the octagonal tower with coloured bulbs like a 21st birthday party at a country hall. People in Hobart are still inordinately proud of the casino even though every other state now has at least one.

As far as police activity goes, Sandy Bay was relatively quiet for drug activity as the rental prices were a bit steep. Drug dealers are rather keen on keeping business overheads like rent low.

However, one place a few blocks from the uni had drawn attention to itself by having frequent short-stay visitors, and was scheduled for a visit from the drug squad.

Mid-afternoon seemed to be the best time to find someone at home but persistent knocking on the door had elicited no response.

The Sandy Bay house was two storeys and music coming from an open upper window suggested that the knocking was being ignored. The smallest policewoman was hoisted onto the shoulders of the largest, and she nimbly swung herself over the balcony rail.

'There's someone in there!' she yelled. A foot slammed into the front door and it exploded inward, sending the lock flying into the hallway.

From my position in the street, I could see a man in the upper hallway, momentarily frozen, zip lock bags in his hands. Down the corridor, the door to the toilet stood open. There was a sudden pause. An officer drew his gun and stepped forward into the front door way.

'Police! Don't move!' he boomed. The man half turned to look back at the toilet, as if gauging the distance or his luck.

'He'll have to have guts to go on,' I thought. Shaking, he lowered the bags to the floor as the officer bounded up the stairs and pushed him against the wall. Those of us outside breathed out.

I harnessed Elise up and moved to the front door. I had just given Elise the 'Find it!' command when she stopped suddenly in the entrance, swerving back around me to the balcony, hammering one of a row of large pots lining the path. I slammed the dummy down before Elise tipped the big pot over. 'Good girl!'.

Under an inner pot containing the plant there was a wad of

deal bags of cannabis.

'It's not even in my house!' protested the man.

'You got off lightly, I reckon,' I said to him as we walked back to the car, Elise woofing victoriously.

Boarding parties

Hobart looks its best from the water. You can appreciate how toy-town it looks, hugging the hills below the mountain and the picturesque look of the city harbour. The humpbacked curve of the Tasman Bridge over the Derwent rises lopsidedly up to join the western and eastern shores, and the apparent calm of the water belies the fact that it is very deep.

• • •

In 1975 a cargo ship, the *Lake Illawarra* crashed into the previous bridge and brought it down. People in Hobart tend to forget that the ship is still lying on the bottom under the bridge, containing the unfortunate crew and the occupants of cars that fell into the gap. The channel is so deep that ships now pass over it without danger. What locals like to remember about the bridge collapse is that the car that teetered over the edge was saved, and not just any car, an American Monaro, no less.

• • •

The calm harbour that Hobart was founded on is in sharp contrast to the great expanse of the Southern Ocean brooding just beyond the rolling hills of Bruny Island. Storm Bay at Hobart's south-eastern entrance is named as a warning of what lies beyond. Hobart is home to Australian and French

Antarctic research vessels and is proud of being the Australian gateway to the sub-Antarctic islands and the Antarctic.

In response to the reported plundering of Australian fishing zones by foreign vessels, including the scientific exclusion zones around our sub-Antarctic islands, the government has laid down large sums to create a Southern Ocean patrol.

The Customs Marine patrols off our northern shores sail through the tropics and are often in sight of land. Being out in the perilous seas of the Southern Ocean for months at a time requires seafaring on another level. There are no landfalls except places like McDonald Island, a windswept rocky dome inhabited by seals and penguins.

A Customs patrol boat chased a Uruguayan vessel, which had been caught fishing illegally for six weeks – the fishing boat simply refused to stop. They knew the Customs vessel was unarmed so radio calls and red flags didn't scare them. They were eventually apprehended by armed South African fisheries and Royal Navy vessels off the coast of South Africa.

Consequently, Customs had decided to arm their vessels with twin 50 calibre machine guns.

The SOMPRU (Southern Ocean Marine Patrol and Rescue Unit) vessel *Oceanic Viking* docked in Hobart before its next long patrol in the towering winter seas to the south. I had expected the vessel to be the size of the average ocean fishing craft, but was impressed when I first sighted its blue and yellow livery. It was as large as the Australian Antarctic ship *Aurora Australis*. It would have to be, as the Viking also sailed to the Antarctic on summer patrols.

Having one of 'our' own ships in Hobart was a perfect opportunity to do some ship search training runs with Elise, unrestricted by problems with dog-shy foreign crew or the protocols of taking drugs on board. After a little conversation with the helpful bosun, I was given the use of a couple of corridors of cabins and a group of the crew on their tea break in the mess. They cheerfully lined up for a simulated passive search exercise and being able to hide drugs in the cabins as I wished was a pleasant change.

The sailing staff were contracted from P&O to operate the ship and all the boarding stuff was done by Customs and Fisheries officers. Apparently the difficulty in having both Customs and non-Customs staff on board was that the department liked to keep the *Viking's* missions secret. The sailing staff were not told where and for how long they would be going until the last moment to 'preserve security', making it difficult for them to stay in contact with families.

The *Viking* departed Hobart for its mission into the Southern Ocean.

I knew something was up when my supervisor was called to meetings with a succession of unannounced visitors from Central office, and then asked me mysteriously whether I was available on the weekend for 'some work I can't discuss just yet'.

The *Oceanic Viking* had captured a vessel believed to have been fishing off McDonald Island and was escorting it to Hobart. The known details were that the ship was Cambodian registered and had a crew of mostly eastern European origin. I had said to the *Vikings'* Bosun that no doubt the government would want to get some return on their couple of hundred million dollars investment in the form of some impressive publicity about SOMPRU pursuing and boarding ships, and, most importantly, recording it all on camera for publicity.

The Customs PR people were some of the first to arrive and were working the phones, the laptops and the spin to make sure it all looked good for the Saturday arrival under the guns.

Immigration were to take charge of the crew, pending decisions by Fisheries about their culpability. In the meantime they were to be disembarked to an unspecified location – Tasmania's Guantanamo Bay – and out of media range.

Customs would then perform a search before handing the ship and its catch over to Fisheries, with interested parties the Department of Transport and the AFP also on hand. The many departments with their various angles would of course bring the expected bureaucratic tangling.

The weather on that Saturday was bleak, overcast and showery. With so many departments falling over each other, the plan to have the crew processed by lunchtime was quickly abandoned and Customs were still completing their boarding requirements well into Saturday night. By Sunday the weather had turned to fog and persistent rain and with 50 tons of illegal catch in the holds, the ship stank.

After the briefings of the search teams from the *Viking*, I established that the crew themselves were not of any other interest to Customs for drugs, and as the ship had been out of port for months and under escort for the last three days, the chances of there being any drugs on board were remote. Customs, however, needed to make sure they had left no stone unturned before they handed the vessel over to AFMA, lest it cause us some interdepartmental embarrassment.

At least I could save Elise and myself the considerable and unnecessary effort of searching the 26 cabins, as the crew had removed their baggage when they left and were unlikely to have left something incriminating behind. The search teams would be going through each cabin anyway, so I concentrated my efforts on the communal stores, messes, locker rooms, workshops and holds, taking note of the many loose fish hooks left lying around from hauling in the catch.

The fishing ship looked like a rust bucket on the outside, but inside it was actually quite well kept and clean. The marine engineers from the *Viking* said that the engines were in good shape, as you would want them to be if you were thousands of miles from any port and in high seas. The exterior condition made sense, as in the Southern Ocean the Antarctic conditions are such that there is no time or place to be scraping and painting the outside, especially when there's illegal fishing to be done.

I made sure Elise was wearing her protective 'Muttluk' sled dog boots, to save her from a hook through the paw, and we swept through the ship. She did show a few unusual changes in behaviour in areas like the toilet cubicles and engine room workshop, but nothing was found after the enthusiastic search team had been through.

They did turn up an impressive collection of multi-lingual, multi-cultural porn, including one Spanish language edition featuring a model sitting naked on the back of a Galapagos tortoise in its island habitat. These boys had definitely been away for a while, and it looked like they might be for a while longer.

We left the impounded fishing vessel for Fisheries, the courts and history to decide, and Customs happily broadcast their footage and stills of the fishing boat seen over the barrel of a .50 calibre with the armed boarding party racing up rope ladders from their zodiacs. Money seen to being well spent.

• • •

While staff at the Hobart office were away on courses, we were joined by a Tasmania-based SOMPRU officer who had opted to work from his home port rather than spend another six weeks at sea. A cheerful bear of a man, he brought a welcome connection to the seas that were just visible from the small office in Hobart.

He fascinated everyone with his tales of a different side of the department – armed boarding, machine gun practice, visits to the volcanos and the penguin colonies of Heard and McDonald Islands. SOMPRU was like a completely different department altogether, only vaguely under the Customs banner, and recruited people unlike Customs officers to perform roles unlike Customs.

The officer had seen service in Iraq with a Navy diving team, had been to the Antarctic several times with ANARE, and had been on patrols with French Fisheries from Madagascar as the lowest-ranked officer in SOMPRU.

He was amazed by the penny pinching that occurred in 'normal' Customs – managers trying to stop officers claiming one hour of overtime and constantly bleating that we were over budget. He came from a department where officers were flown wherever they were needed, paid 24 hours a day and expected to perform under all conditions and circumstances.

The line between the two departments was brought into sharp contrast when Customs officers did the arrival boarding functions on a SOMPRU vessel returning from international waters. They found that the SOMPRU officers had souvenired some of the empty, expended .50 calibre shell casings from firing practice, and threatened to charge them with importing prohibited weapons of war, even though the ammunition came from Australia. It was a case of the bean counters striking back.

• • •

Boarding is a Customs function to clear the documents, certificates and procedures of the ship, its cargo and crew for arrival and departure. Previously it was a job for those with an eye for detail on paperwork who could also hold their drink – they did the paperwork while the ship's officers plied them with booze. In the old days, there was a mountain of paperwork and much more drinking – it was an accepted seafaring way of doing business with government officials. The old naval term 'Boarding party' had a celebratory meaning for Customs boarding officers.

Now such activities are labelled as an OH&S and a Probity issue.

It's a sign of how the world has changed that boarding officers were some of the first Customs officers to be given guns, as 'the first line of counter-terrorism defence' in an obscure Government announcement. The world was certainly changed by September the 11 attacks.

In Tasmania, '9/11' is the name of a chain of bottle shops, not as some misguided monument to the attacks in New York but as an indication of its opening hours. Well, I suppose Melbourne has a Harold Holt Memorial Swimming Pool, one of the local pools where I grew up (Harold Holt was Prime

Minister of Australia before he disappeared in December 1967 while swimming in the sea and was presumed drowned).

A weekend operation to search an Iranian bulk carrier had the added interest of the ship anchoring overnight in the Derwent, waiting for a free berth. If we waited until it docked, any contraband aboard could easily have been off loaded onto a small craft in the night, or dropped over the side to be collected. That may, of course, have happened anywhere along the coast, but it was decided to board it at anchorage.

Despite much grumbling from the cops that it was a weekend and involved OT, they agreed to supply two boats and crews to watch the ship and run the search team out to it. Finally, I might get a chance to do the sort of boarding we had practised in Sydney. I took out my pack of climbing ropes, devices and carabiners, strapping Elise into her day-glo support harness and we clambered onto the motorboat tied up at Battery Point.

Despite the drizzle, the river was calm and the ride out in the motorboat was very smooth so the gangway could be lowered to our small boat and instead of us scaling ladders. We boarded by stepping off the deck on to the gangway steps. I clipped Elise to me using carabiners to link our harnesses in case she slipped, but other than that there was little difference from walking up the gangway from the wharf.

The search proceeded as normal. I waited on deck while the captain was consulted and the crew mustered in the mess room. Elise swept down the laughing and groaning line of men, smelling of tobacco, sweat and grease. She swung back and forth nosing around their legs without paying anyone particular attention.

A master key was secured from the Bosun and the search

team unlocked lockers and stores for Elise to search, in lieu of any specific information about an individual to be the target of the search. Ships are usually quite hot inside the accommodation block and after giving Elise a restorative rest and a drink out on the deck, we searched the empty cabins and common areas like games rooms, workshops and laundry. Nothing of interest occurred, except for a race between the Police boats taking us back.

Everyone stepped back onto Battery Point flushed, smiling and excited at the end of a good day out.

CHAPTER 8

UNCONSCIOUS CUES

A dog is a labour-saving device

The Western District-Devonport Drug Squad had a case they hadn't been able to crack, and hoped Elise could do it. A house in East Devonport, near the *Spirit of Tasmania* Ferry terminal, had been searched twice over the last months after complaints from parents that their children had apparently bought cannabis from there on their way home from high school. The owner denied all knowledge and was what they described as a 'crafty old bugger' with a long criminal history.

'If it's grass there really isn't much he could do to hide it from the dog,' I pronounced confidently. 'Except if it's up in the roof maybe,' I added, with a note of caution.

I followed the police over to the quiet street of weatherboards. The owner was indeed more than old enough to know better, and had a sarcastic look on his face when he opened the door.

'Youse again! Ya wasting ya time. I don't know what those kids tell ya but I've got nothin'.' he barked. The police nodded to me and marched him through to the back porch of the small house. I had a quick look inside and noted that the room was hot from a blazing wood stove in the middle of the open kitchen/lounge, making a note to keep Elise away.

'Who's that bloke?' I heard the man asking.

'He's got the dog, Bert!' said the Drug Squad Sergeant Elise was racing to get in and leapt off the front steps through the open door, immediately veering erratically around the room as if pulled by an invisible cord.

'Everyone stand back!' I called as I did my best to stop her contacting the hot stove. She collided with the kitchen cupboards at the back of the room and frantically scratched at the floor as she pushed her nose along the woodwork. I pulled open the cupboard door and her paws crashed into the cups, scattering them as she hammered at the wooden base. 'Good girl!' I cried, desperately pulling her back from the cupboard with big pats on the chest.

The owner's face appeared frozen in alarm through the kitchen window.

I knew I would have a tough time getting her away from such a strong odour to search the rest of the room, but Elise suddenly took off toward the open front door. I stumbled to keep control of her and to work out what was happening. She veered right, toward the stove and as I tried to pull her way she rounded the back and attacked the pile of neatly stacked spilt timber. Wood thumped to the floor and she concentrated on the big log at the bottom. I pulled it away from the stove and saw a loose chunk had shifted from a hollow. I slammed the dummy down as Elise lunged for the stash and she cut circles around the lounge shaking it furiously in triumph.

While I praised her lavishly, the constable searching the kitchen cupboard gave me the thumbs up with his blue gloved hands, pointing to the ounce bags of cannabis laid out under the false floor with a big grin.

It had taken them hours on previous searches without result. Elise had taken seconds to locate the two stashes.

'Probably the best thirty seconds of work we've done, hey Elise?' I said proudly.

An unexpected light

I found Tasmania both beautiful and surprising in unexpected ways.

I walked out of a film screening one night to the sight of a bright comet trailing an illuminated feathery tail through the night sky. Walking home, some fire twirlers drew fiery wheels in the air in the Parliament gardens and a group at the dock nearby found that a cast stone sent shimmering ripples of neon blue phosphorescence through the water.

On the way to work one summer morning, a well-dressed group gathered in the corner of St David's park for some mysterious ceremony. The men were dressed in Victorian suits with winged collars and the woman in golden cloaks. A bagpiper skirled a dirge into the early morning quiet. Past them marched a man wearing 70s-era tight football shorts, a pink short-sleeved body shirt with a wide tie, a big moustache and a heavy comb over, not giving the piper at glance and not looking like he had dressed up for a laugh.

The standard of dress for formal occasions is more decidedly casual in Hobart, with wedding invitations specifying 'Neat casual – no polar fleece.'

Locals distinguish themselves by wearing t-shirts on winter mornings, being proud of not owning raincoats or wearing sunhats, despite the skin-sizzlingly high UV due to a Southern Ocean ozone hole. Try as I might, I could not convince friends from Melbourne that Hobart was only marginally colder in winter, and only rarely got above warm in summer.

Driving up the Brooker Highway, a group of wild ladies in red burst out of the domain gardens ahead, bolting across the road. Oh, make that a group of wild men in red dresses, wigs and jogging shoes. Their choice of fashion seemed a little odd so early in the day. Their apparel was suited for nightclubs – sequins, lame and satin – all necessarily short to allow for the free movement of their hairy legs.

The pack leader was a stocky man who pounded along in a risqué red PVC mini-dress, calling directions to the straggling pack of transvestites behind. Other cars slowed down to observe this spectacle.

At a petrol station, I asked the young woman working the pumps if there was any reason a large group of men in red dresses was running through the streets. She reflected and replied slowly, 'Dunno. It's Saturday, I s'pose.'

Was this a normal sight on a Saturday here?

At the kennels, one of the Quarantine service dogs was barking at what I thought was a bone under its bed and began to reach under the bed before deciding to have a look, my eyes were greeted by the open mouth a of a Tiger snake.

CHAPTER 8

It took a fire hose to remove the recalcitrant snake while I pondered the close call. The week previously I had found another tiger snake lying on the sand at the beach. An Aboriginal woman once told me finding a snake was a sign of change. Something to think about!

Out for a walk

An officer from the drug squad called with a request that I take my dog for a walk past a house in the city. He suspected that the place was being used as a hydroponic cannabis growing house, and considering Elise's previous success in identifying another hydro house in north Hobart, he thought he might get some extra confirmation to enable him to get a warrant.

He told me which house they were interested in and asked if I could get the dog to search the outside of the house without drawing attention to myself.

I put on plain clothes and parked a block away, letting Elise wander sniffing power poles and car tyres until we came to the place, a two- storey house with suspiciously drawn blinds all the way around. I thought for a second I could smell cannabis myself and, checking that I wasn't being observed, let Elise off the lead to run along the front of the house and down the driveway with a quiet 'Find it'.

As she turned the corner down the side of the house, she swung around, drew back under a window sill, rising up on her hind legs scenting the air before continuing on, swinging back a little less below the next window down the descent of the drive. I followed her around the back where I was brought to a halt by the sight of a car and motorbike in the yard, the rear windows uncovered. Watching the window blinds for any sign of movement, I quietly called her back and walked her back to the car.

'Yeah, change of behaviour around the windows and I could hear the hum of an electrical transformer inside' I told the officer.

'Righto. We'll get a warrant. Thanks!' he responded. The Drug Squad had good reason to trust Elise's instincts as she had shown them some concealed drugs that they had admitted they would have been hard pressed to find.

Two weeks later the house was entered, surprising two men inside along with 80 plants, four and a half kilos of cannabis and 12 ecstasy tablets. I didn't feel wholly responsible for the bust and was reluctant to claim the contents as a 'dog' seizure.

I drove past a house in Lutana that another officer wanted us to check out, parking a few blocks away and joining the other dog walkers coming to and from the park on a cool, sunny day.

It's surprising how abnormal and conspicuous this felt, even though I knew Elsie and I were indistinguishable.

Elise pissed on front lawns like a normal dog, but I could see that there was now a car in front of the target premises. The front of the target house was set well back from the street at the top of a steeply sloped front yard. It would have been too obvious to walk right up to the house.

I stroked a few hairs from Elise's back and released them, checking the wind direction. The wind was blowing from behind the house, and I thought that there might be a chance Elise would run up herself to investigate if she picked up any scent. As we came to the front of the property I unclipped her and hissed, 'Find it!'

Elise was jerked from her doggy world preoccupation and into work mode, shooting forward with her nose down and sniffing intently along the edge of the garage roller door that met the pavement. She traced back and forth at the base of the door with unusual intensity. I glanced up and down the street while deciding I would tell the police she was 'closely interested' in the garage.

My attention was snapped back by a sound like rocks on a tin roof, the hammering of her paws scratching against the corrugated metal door.

'Oh! Good girl!' I said as loudly as I dared, hoping there was no one in the garage to hear me. She lunged forward again and I tore the miniature 'undercover' dummy from my pocket and tossed it against the door. She snatched it up and as I clipped her back onto the lead, another car drew up in front of the house, pulling in beside us.

'Oh, what a funny dog,' I said, trying to estimate what a normal pet owner would say when playing fetch.

I glanced to the side but didn't think the driver had seen anything unusual. We walked rapidly back to the car and I phoned the officer with the report of the positive response, A few weeks later he confirmed that the garage housed a hydroponic set up, but although the floor was covered in scraps of cannabis, the plants had gone. At least it wasn't a stash of Elise's favourite dog food in the garage.

Done bikin'

Two premises searches for 'speed' were requested for the unusual time of an evening mid-week. Almost every other job was done in the morning – drug people are usually out on business at night.

I sat around the kennels after hours, waiting for the call. The Drug Squad instructed me to drive down to the southern satellite seaside town of Kingston and wait around the shopping centre area for further instructions.

I found a spot near the park in a quiet street until the phone rang again to call me to the house.

After some initial confusion as to which flat in the block the cops were actually in, I entered a neat unit at the end of the drive, the interior unremarkable except for the Nazi daggers decorating the wall. Big Brother on TV droned its mediocrity into the lounge while a pot-bellied man in a Harley Davidson t-shirt and a grey ponytail sat on the couch, chatting with the detectives in their suits and ties.

The term 'mate' seemed to be used very frequently in the conversation, considering that it was about his drug habits and the 20 or so deals of speed on the kitchen table. The outcome of the evening was obviously going to be less than friendly to him.

I asked the police to remove the bag of deals, so there was less drug odour to distract Elise when searching the house for what they hadn't found, but believed was hidden somewhere.

Elise strained at the lead as we entered the door, swinging to and fro in room swirling with drug odours. She responded strongly to an open book lying on a low shelf, and I praised her enthusiastically, and was told by the police that each page had held a deal like an index.

Johnny's back was too troublesome to ride a Harley any more so he had opted for driving the less rebellious Mercedes coupe that sat in the garage.

Elise alerted to the outside of the car and was threatening to jump through the window as I held her back to open the door. Inside, she immediately traced the source to the centre console around the shift and manically scratched at the panel.

Seeing her confident response, I flicked her dummy onto the spot and called for the detectives to check out that place.

'We have, mate. I'll show you' said one of the suits. He leant in and pulled back the panel with the rip of Velcro, revealing a shelf underneath.

'That's where he deals from. Shame you couldn't find any more, but the dog seems to be going well.' he offered.

I was heartened by Elise's strong identification of the smell of local 'speed' as it seemed to confirm the validity of her training. I returned Elise to the car to tear up her dummy and began helping the police to manually search the kitchen.

I was called to go to a second address immediately, a house in upper Glenorchy, which meant driving back into Hobart and along the roads along the lower slopes of Mt Wellington. I wasn't familiar with the area and there were a lot of winding and dead end streets. I took at least four wrong turns and an extra 20 minutes before finally seeing the line of marked and unmarked police cars outside the large weatherboard.

The Drug Squad were sitting in the big back shed looking dejected. The house belonged to the parents of a bike gang associate of the gentleman who had just been busted, and both boys visited frequently and kept bikes and parts in the sheds.

The police believed that they used the parent's home as a safe house for hiding drugs, possibly burying the speed in the backyard in metal screw-capped cylinders. I was shown an empty one they had found at the first house. They had already thoroughly searched the place without success.

I harnessed Elise up and we swung into action in the dark backyard, while I held a torch in one hand and the lead in the other. It was a well- tended and weed-free garden, doted on by a retired couple and all the more difficult to search as the beds were regularly 'turned over' by the attentive gardeners.

No joy there.

Entering the house, I found the police talking quietly with a white haired old couple – a postcard-perfect dear old Anglo mum and dad. Their home was neat and cats lazed luxuriously on the chairs, but despite this domestic serenity, I began to get the idea that all was not as it seemed.

In the kitchen was a large farmed picture of a bike gang lined up on their 'hogs', all beards, sneers and tattoos. No doubt their beloved boy was one of them.

I had the cats taken outside to the shed and the old couple seated in the kitchen with the police before I brought Elise in. I swept around the rooms with Elise searching, noticing odd items lying around that alarmed me.

In a wicker basket with sewing gear sat a set of brass knuckles, next to the photo albums was a can of teargas, a long dagger lay on a pile of Reader's Digests and a Nazi flag lay half covered by a pile of magazines. Well, perhaps they weren't like everyone else's old folks.

A police video unit officer was there, filming proceedings for evidence, and I told him to keep out of the dog's way.

Elise charged out of the lounge into the corridor a couple of times, as if finding and losing some thin trail of odour. Entering one of the spare bedrooms, she quickly found it again, swerving into a corner filled with a rack of old coats and handbags, jumping at them. I let her pull down some bags and waited until she began pawing at one before subbing in her dummy.

The police called in the old lady. 'Are these your bags?' they asked

'Oh yes, but I don't use them now' she smiled.

They opened the black handbag and inside was an ounce of cannabis heads in a zip lock bag.

'Oh, I've never seen that before!' she exclaimed.

After seeing the dangerous 'decorations' around the house I wasn't so sure. The officer who had searched that room before my arrival was shamefaced and admitted he now owed a six-pack to his squad for his lack of attention.

I never saw a drink of that, but I was proud of Elise. We had come on as a house bust team in leaps and bounds.

To catch a dream

At the kennels, I decided to sort out the previous handlers' accumulation of papers and junk in the rarely cleaned filing cabinets, using the waste to fill boxes and bags for training exercises.

Folded up in an envelope was a yellowing newsprint clipping headlining a drug search of the *Spirit of Tasmania* ferry in 1994. The banner screamed,

'Ferry drugs raid. 80 police, customs with sniffer dogs arrest crew'.

I thought it worthy of framing, as no one could remember any other paper headline involving Customs, and considering that the issue of drugs brought over on the ferry was again a political issue in Tassie.

The state opposition had managed to grab local media attention on this issue several times in a few weeks, but getting that sort of attention wasn't hard considering that the Hobart newspaper The Mercury often had very little to make into a headline. The Mercury loved a pun and boasted such headlines as 'Maccas roasts Tassie spuds' in reference to the McDonalds Corporation claiming that the local potatoes were substandard for use in their esteemed food. I think I saw a man being borne on the shoulders of a cheering throng issuing from the Mercury office on the day of that pun, bearing its author straight to the bar of Montgomery's to celebrate his finest hour.

While buying a picture frame for the ferry banner at Chickenfeed, the now defunct Tasmanian Walmart, the checkout chick looked closely at the Customs crest on my fleece jacket and struck up a conversation.

'Customs eh? Do you have a dog?' she asked eagerly.

I thought her keen eye had detected the white dog hair covering my dark blue uniform, but found that an expectant public ask that of every officer down here.

'I guess you have the beagle at the airport?' she pressed.

'No, actually the beagles search for fruit for Quarantine, and I have a Labrador to search for drugs' I explained. The Quarantine officers continually got asked if they were doing a drug bust.

While explaining the difference between Quarantine and Customs, I remembered the close connection between some of the best-selling décor items at Chickenfeed and the Tasmanian criminal aesthetic.

'In almost every drug house I raid with the police, the dealers always have 'Chickenfeed' dream catchers, with American Indian and dolphin designs. Take a good look at anyone buying dream catchers, as they're sure to be a druggie' I enlightened the shop assistant.

She beamed with delight at this information and as there were no customers waiting, ran off to tell her workmates. 'Hey, listen to this!' she called, dashing across the shop.

Later I went to a premises search in Launceston, the target a woman known to be running a 'mixed business' – dealing speed and prostitution – all apparently from her bedroom. The sign at the door, telling everyone to take their shoes off or wait outside, suggested a frequency of visitors.

Suspended from the ceiling was the Earth Mother of all dream catchers, a big catcher the size of a basketball with four or five smaller ones dangling from its hoop. It was a sure sign that there would be drugs in there and in this case the power of the dream catcher also told their location – right underneath it. Elise swung onto a tin on the floor which was found to contain a wad of deal bags, a set of scales and about five grams of speed.

Perhaps the police didn't need a dog to tell them where the stuff was if they used their eyes … and followed their dreams.

Down on the farm

Prisons called to ask me to search the prison farm at Hayes again. Drugs were coming in during the weekend contact visits and the security section planned to hit the prison on a Saturday night when the prisoners would be holding. Instead of searching the cells and work areas, this time their plan was to search the prisoners, or rather for Elise and I to do it for them.

I disliked having any contact with the prisoners, but the security section assured me that they would bring them in small groups of a dozen or so and immediately take away anyone the dog reacted to. We would then search that prisoner's cell while the rest were kept away.

It was a sunny, still evening and the prisoners were mustered in a main assembly yard for the last roll call of the day. Security interrupted this routine to read the 'Riot act', telling the inmates to stand in lines, not to move, talk or attempt to interfere with the dog in any way, as doing so would result in the immediate removal of all privileges and return to Risdon prison.

There were 75 men lined up and only eight prison officers so I was apprehensive about what would happen if trouble started. Security thought it unlikely, but added 'if anything happens, lock yourself and the dog in the car.' Great!

I walked Elise up the five long lines of smirks, sneers and sidelong glances and commanded her to 'Find it!' Elise searched well, working methodically along the avenue of legs, and I fought to keep my eyes on her.

I was surprised that the prisoners stood so still, and even the expected profanity and threats didn't happen. On the contrary, these boys stood in very straight lines, even shuffling back to let Elise pass unchecked and only hissed jokes and sniggering rippled through the ranks. Despite a very close and attentive search, Elise only changed behaviour to one bloke, nosing his right pocket very specifically. I praised her and pointed him out to the security officers, and he was led away to be searched, to jokes and cheers. There wasn't anything on him and the officers looked disappointed at the lack of result.

The passive search turned out to be the easy part as I then had to push her, with much invented enthusiasm on my part, to search a block of 20 cells. That also showed no result and so we then went onto the same milking and hay sheds where we had found the 'needle in the haystack'. This time there was nothing. The expressions of the officers suggested that they thought we had missed something. I had done my best, and Elise even better than that.

Due to the extent of the searches Elise had been doing at the prison farm, I thought it wise to set up some training and reward exercises there, as we were sure to be working there again and I wanted to maintain Elise's motivation. I asked the prison security unit to tee up another day with the farm management, and advised them that I would need an area of the sheds and a row of cells for the training to be worthwhile.

I had prepared some small items like a matchbox, and envelope and a piece of metal pipe scented with the odours of Ecstasy, heroin and cocaine to use in there, not wishing to take any real drugs into that environment. Under my direction, the officers placed the envelope under a mattress, the matchbox with like objects on a shelf above the standard cell desk, and the pipe with other metal items in the shed. Having them handle and place the articles helped to maintain some realism and the dog's focus on finding the odour alone in context with the usual things found in those areas.

The purpose of using two stims (training stimulus) in the cells was to do a 'praise off and work on' exercise with Elise, giving her praise instead of a dummy and then encouraging her to work on through several more cells before locating a different odour and then being rewarded with a dummy. This is to keep her working after a first alert in operations, when the expectation is that we 'clear' areas in spite of early success. Elise hopefully then understood that if she kept working after the praise off, there would be a dummy coming later.

I just knew that prisons would try and sneak in a few operational requests on us while we were there and they didn't disappoint.

'Could you just do this guy's cell first? We'd really like to get him with something.' asked the female officer. I figured I needed a row of cells anyway to make it realistic and this may as well be one of them.

The officers stood in an expectant semi-circle around the door as Elise searched, but she wasn't interested in the cell, and I shook my head as I moved on to the next. After the last search at Hayes I had the impression that they may have had more faith in their informants than in Elise, but let it pass.

It was interesting watching her head flicks as she passed the mattress with the scented envelope under it, a thin stream of target odour in the room. I enacted the drill of pivoting her to where her head flicked and pumped the mattress to expel more odour, at which she fixed herself to the ungainly task of trying to paw the bed from underneath. I pulled her back slowly and firmly while praising her and kept her attention on the reward as we backed out of the cell, then led her straight into the next cell to work on. She did so without complaint, and we moved on to the next blank cell, but it wasn't so blank.

Elise jumped up on the lower bunk and rose up on her hind legs, sniffing intently along the tubular metal frame and wagging her tail furiously. I grabbed her harness and drew her back down, praising her again with thumping pats on the chest as we left the cell in reverse.

'In there, the bunk. Full search, thanks.' I requested the officers, who looked surprised.

The officers found that a wooden plug had been inserted in the tubular bunk frame to stop any items from dropping down irretrievably. In side were only a couple of deals of cannabis, but enough to send the inmate back to the main prison. It was a good 'hide' and one they hadn't been expecting, in the bunk of someone they hadn't suspected. I always think surprises are sweetest when they are illicit.

CHAPTER 9

OLFACTORY ACUITY

Nothing to do today

My daily routine, along with any searches of freight for Customs, was to maintain and develop all Elise's abilities with constant training exercises.

The exercises were necessary to provide the dog with a tangible reward in areas where we were not getting hits, which was just about everywhere except house searches. If a dog doesn't locate a target odour and get a reward in a particular area, say in sea freight, then its interest in searching sea freight will gradually decline until it is hardly searching at all. It will still search well in the other areas in which it is receiving reward, as the idea of where and when it is rewarded is very task and location specific.

Similarly, if a dog is rewarded frequently in one freight

shed, and not at all in another, then it will save its energy for searching in the shed where reward occurs.

The goal of training is to maintain the idea that a reward may come at anywhere and at any time in the dog's mind so it is always searching at its best, no matter the location or circumstances. This must be balanced against extending the dog's intent and capabilities in all areas and keeping the training realistic and without consistent characteristics that may get the dog focussed on finding training articles rather than the real and unexpected target. Good training requires planning, resourcefulness, objectivity and an element of risk.

Reward isn't the only reason training exercises are performed, as sometimes it is to test the dog's ability by making the presentation of drug odours difficult or unusual, just to see what the dog will do and which level it is at.

I had been having some difficulty with Elise's identification of the crystal methyl-amphetamine or ice. She either didn't recognise its smell at all, or just showed a small amount of interest in basic presentations. I had tried taking her back to the most basic type of run with the maximum quantity of ice sitting in an open slatted crate, and after several seconds of deep sniffing she was able to decide for herself that the odd chemical smell was one of her target odours, and scratch at the crate. However, as soon as the same drug was placed into a mail parcel she seemed to hardly recognise it – just a few flicks of the head. Compared to other drugs, ice has relatively little odour, but we were also using relatively large amounts in training.

Elise's identification of ice noticeably improved after contact with the local types of amphetamines produced by Tasmania's friendly bike gangs. Somehow the stronger smell of the powder amphetamines helped her to find the subtle odours of the crystalline variety.

One of the scenarios for assisting police with premises searches involved looking for quantities of drugs buried in a backyard or property. Training exercises had to be done to ensure that if Elise was pointed towards a patch of bush and told to find it, she would work with her nose close to the ground and investigate all the rocks, holes, paving stones and other features under which her target odour, and therefore her reward, could be concealed. To bury something involved giving the odour time to permeate out from the earth, so training aids had to be left overnight, at least.

Obviously, leaving real drugs in an unsecured area overnight is a no-no – I would be sacked, if not charged, if the training aid disappeared. The problem is that articles that have been scented by their proximity to drugs rapidly lose their odour in cool, moist environments and may be rendered odourless by dawn the next day.

I chose a roadside reserve east of the airport with an embankment that hid me from the highway, burying an empty jar in one side of the gully as a control.

To be sure of the reason the dog found the drugs, controls, similar jars and plastic bags without any drug odour, must be used. I then dug a series of holes on each side of the gully to give Elise plenty of places to investigate and to ensure that disturbed ground was not the reason for her finding the training aid.

I carefully placed the training aid into a half-dug rabbit hole with as little disturbance as possible. It contained some plastic bags that had been used on my cannabis stocks, and I opened the lid of the jar a touch to slowly release the odour.

We returned the next day. I quickly harnessed Elise and directed her to search along the gully. She sniffed the place of the control jar and walked on, more interested in other patches I had disturbed. I swung her over to the other side of the gully to work toward the training aid but just before she got to the rabbit hole, she picked her head up and swung away from the line of search, bounding over to where the control jar was buried and unhesitatingly digging away at it.

I corrected her with a sharp 'No!' and took her straight back to the car as a sign of disapproval, game over.

It was like she had been thinking about noticing the control and had just put it together by the time she was on the other side of the gully. Back to the drawing board.

I returned a few days later to a new area with a jar that had been used for cocaine storage and a coke-scented dummy that had been in the safe a long time, along with a totally clean jar as a control. They were concealed under the bushes about 20 m apart, the lid of the coke jar locked down to retain the odour until needed.

After two weeks of rain and sun, I visited briefly to check they were still in place and popped open the lids of both jars with the aid of a stick, so my hand scent did not flag their presence.

All was set for the training the next day, but to make Elise believe we were far from home, I took her on a little drive in the country. We cut a circuit out through the historic town of Richmond, heavy with antique shops and cream tea places, and back in from the east through the satellite town of Sorell.

At the site Elise pulled eagerly on her harness but a loud

clucking and a flurry of feathers announced that we had invaded the territory of two wild and apparently angry chickens. Elise lunged at them sending then squawking off, but her ears and tail stayed erect and her attention was directed to the bushes they had flapped behind. She was no longer interested in following my commands. I couldn't complain that realistic distractions weren't included in the training.

I circled her around to show her the fowl had flown, and then gave her a forceful command to search. She ran with her nose down and passed by the bush containing the blank jar without changing behaviour, but just as we were coming up to the stimulus, she was distracted by an outraged squawk and swung away to try and grab some free chicken lunch. Bugger. I pulled her back to the line of search but we were now past the training aid and I worked her on to search the bushes on the other side of the track, deciding to make her work for longer and take a second pass.

She again swung away from the line of search and as I readied to correct her for chasing the chooks, she veered straight on to the bush with the target beneath it and scratched furiously at the branches, diving under to emerge with the coke scented dummy in her mouth and leaping for joy. 'Good girl!' I cheered, hoping that it proved more rewarding than catching a chicken.

Back at the office, when asked what I had been doing lately. I replied, 'Oh, just a training run.'.

It may not sound much like work to anyone else, but it was mine.

Back to the future

I was requested for some premises searches at Sorell, which seemed a little close to home for me. Sorell was really a country town fast becoming a satellite suburb of Hobart and it was also the next suburb from Midway Point where I was house sitting. The only thing I knew about Sorell was that it had been the birthplace of the legendary combat cameraman Neil Davis, who made his mark in the Vietnam War. Davis once described the American tactic of bombarding a suspected Vietcong village as being 'like destroying Sorell in order to get rid of a few undesirable elements', a tactic also possibly considered by the local cops.

Living in Hobart with its relatively small population means encountering the same people constantly.

The police had a system of allowing officers to opt out of working in their own suburbs, as long as a substitute could be arranged. In later years, I also had reason to ask not to be included on a premises search around the corner from where I was living.

We met at the Sorell police station, a gathering of the drug squad and local cops, under the paternalistic gaze of the Area Inspector.

A local cop with a broken nose and heavily tattooed arms had done some sterling research on one of the local crims who was a big marijuana grower, seller and gambler, reputedly spending up to $2000 a week on the pokies. He had been turned over two years before but was back to his old tricks. The suspect was a large man, a sort of Sorell Meatloaf.

The two houses targeted were the crim's home, a newish house in the re-developed area of the town, and his parents' place, right by the main street shops. I was asked to go to the old folks' place first, and they were none too pleased at having their lunch preparations disrupted and having to open their many sheds of junk to the visitors.

The police sat the parents down in the kitchen and nodded for Elise to begin work.

The house was a neat, old place with faded curtains and carpets but Elise was very interested in the saggy central seat of the couch and a jumper in the spare bedroom. I praised her heartily and pointed to the couch and jumper for searching. Nothing was visible but the parents confirmed that both items had been in contact with their beloved son, as I suspected.

Most of the block was filled with a double row of sheds and garages facing each other across a drive, and our suspect had set up clubhouses in a couple of these, housing car and motorbike parts, a collection of video parlour games, two bars, several jukeboxes, a display of stuffed animals from deer to mongooses, and a three kg sack of dope in the storeroom.

He wasn't home, but his father showed the police the sack, knowing they would have found it anyway. The clubhouse area stunk of cannabis, so there was little point in taking Elise in there. It was difficult enough to get her to search even two sheds away as she was swinging towards the target odour.

I told the Police that under the circumstances, they would have to do a manual search as the odour of cannabis from the storeroom was too strong.

The suspect's father, not quite as tubby as his son, stood outside with the Police.

'Is that the same dog that was here last time you buggers came?' he asked.

'No, this is our first visit. Why, what happened to the other dog?' I asked, cautiously

'Oh, it ate some rat poison in the shed'.

'How long ago?'

'Oh, about two years, maybe'.

I had never heard about this and thought he might have been confusing Customs with someone else.

An intelligence officer back at the office confirmed that he had been helping the previous handler on a search at the same place, and her dog had scarfed down some Ratsak and had had to be rushed to the vet. She survived.

No one was home at the suspect's residence. The police had entered regardless, recording the events on video and with the attendance of the Inspector to confirm that all was above board.

I stepped out of the car and immediately was struck by the smell of cannabis, while still five metres from the front door. I got back in and moved the vehicle away to limit Elise's exposure to the gust of target odour.

One of the bathrooms had been converted into a hydro set up, holding maybe a dozen large plants. The set-up had been consuming over $1000 of power a quarter and was a dead give away. Surely the neighbours could smell it from their lounge room as well? There was nothing they needed a dog to find or indeed that she could have found with that smell.

Two days later, the Drug Squad asked me to go back to the parent's place, as their informants swore that much of the stash had been missed by the police. With the three kg bag gone, it was only a little easier to search as there was still much remnant odour in the shed. Elise zoomed around the room, drawing in the heavily laden air and odour from the bits and pieces of 'grass' scattered around. She swung back and forth several times around one of the jukeboxes before settling on attacking a cardboard box.

The box only contained traces of cannabis but the jukebox was full. The locked base of it was levered open to reveal another two kilos all packaged up for sale.

The suspect sat silent and deflated, probably wondering who had dobbed him in. Caught for the second time in two years this was not ideal. In spite of the risk the profits were obviously too good to ignore – and he had a gambling habit and a dead animal collection to support.

To fight another day

Prisons had received information regarding visitors bringing drugs into Risdon on contact visits again and were keen for us to search the weekend visitors. I wasn't, but I had done many training exercises with Elise using the children of staff and friends to try to overcome her fear of small people, and encouraged children to pat her in the park to promote positive contact for Elise. Hopefully, she should now search the lines of visitors whether they were children or adults, but I still regarded working at Risdon as an unfortunate part of my role.

One security officer's 'inside sources' had suggested that drugs had been brought in 'when the Customs dog was on board' by wrapping the contraband in pepper and chilli powder. When asked for my reaction, I said I doubted it. I hadn't done a visitor search for months, and it seemed strange that such important information would come in so late, and also because the use of these types of so-called 'masking agents' may work on Beverley Hills cop, but actually don't deter sniffer dogs.

The dog's ability to discriminate between odours is as superior as its ability to detect them, and strong smells of spices and coffee actually make a person or article more interesting to the dog.

Security had targeted a couple of visitors on the contact visitor list for the Sunday, which also happened to be the first day of Tasmania's early daylight saving period. Daylight saving occurred six weeks ahead of the mainland, I think to stretch out the tourist season. I didn't really care to spend weekends at work, particularly not at the prison. As the weather was fine, I would rather be out bushwalking, but I couldn't complain about the overtime.

I attended at Risdon about 30 minutes before the first visit time, and signed in to be allowed through the double gates and to lock the vehicle out of sight in a cargo bay.

There were supposed to be 20 people in the 10.30 group of visitors, but only eight turned up, the result of the one-hour time change that morning throwing out schedules. The 'real' time was only 9.30, and on a Sunday morning there wasn't enough time to get children organised to come.

Elise happily searched the small line-up of adults, and stopped and sat confidently in front of a woman after nosing her pocket.

The officers escorted her outside and the rest of the group went on with their visits. Unfortunately, she had no drugs on her, but after a body search by a female prison officer, admitted to having 'a few joints' the night before.

There were supposed to be 30 people in the next visit group an hour later, and this time 12 appeared, Security put this down to the word going out from the previous visitors that the dog was searching today.

I soon learned that all the 'child friendly' training exercises I had done made little impression on Elise. She would search larger kids of about six and over, but she avoided the little tackers, making a wide berth around them that was obvious. Oh shit. I felt we had covered most of the visitors except the two small children, but knew that her phobia remained unchanged.

On the last run of visitors in the afternoon I had a sinking feeling the moment I heard a screaming toddler across the yard. A little girl was giving it the full lung and Elise was already baulking and pulling away from the gate rather than towards it. She slunk around the line-up and would barely go near any of the visitors while the child was screaming. I didn't even bother taking her down that end of the line and signalled to the attendant prison officers that the run was finished.

As I walked her back to the car, Elise brightened immediately, and I told the security officers that our days of searching visitors were over. We would still do all the other types of searches on cells, prisoners and the farm, but no more visitors. I conferred with the Canberra Training Centre and they offered to re-team me with another dog if I wished, but advised me that they would shortly be training a team for Tasmanian Corrections anyway, due to plans to build a new prison at Risdon.

Otherwise, Elise was performing very well and the work I had done on ice and amphetamine and local cannabis had improved her ability remarkably. A new dog would have to be trained, a process of several months. As to her welfare as a retired dog, my parents were not able to have another pet just yet, and I didn't want to send her back to the purgatory of being a kennel hound in Canberra after all our work together.

I decided that Elise and I would stay as a team.

Tasmanian Corrections were going ahead with recruiting a dog handler from their ranks to be the first Tasmanian prison dog – a sniffer only, no attack work.

One of their development managers was a former Tasmanian Customs dog handler and instrumental in pushing for prisons to get their own dogs. Customs had agreed to train the dog and handler, to keep up what we regarded as acceptable standards and to enable Customs and Prisons to work together from the same outlook.

I was asked to be on the selection panel, but felt I should instead advise the panel on technical matters as I had to work with the prison officers, not as their superior. I agreed to supervise the practical selection test of taking the applicant through playing a game of tug of war with a dog. A trained dog doing a visual retrieve with an unscented dummy is in effect detraining them, as it encourages the dog to follow visual stimulus and not the unseen stimulus of odour. Consequently, Canberra agreed to fly down one of its demo dogs for the day, and I would set that day aside to take the applicants through the exercise.

First the applicants had to pass the fitness test, the description of which had already reduced the number of applicants from 18 to 11, and after the day of running up and down between marker cones at the Clarence sports centre, six remained, all male.

I picked up DD Kira, again a former Tasmanian dog and was joined by a previous Tassie handler. The taciturn Prison Security manager, made up the third interviewer, and I agreed to sit in on the interview to give a general impression after scoring the applicants' tug of war. I decided to quantify the tug of war as; ability to follow commands, ability to respond, lack of self-consciousness and variety in the game.

I gave each officer an introductory talk and demonstration of how to put on the dog's choker chain and then the harness, walk the dog to the start point, to give it the 'Find it!' command when I threw the dummy and a 'Good girl!' each time the dog picked it up or 'won' the game. I stressed that the game was for the dog to win, and they were to make it fun for the dog, and could say or do as they wished to make it enjoyable for the dog. It is a lot to remember in a very rapid exercise that the dog can easily take in unexpected directions.

The first applicant followed the instructions well enough but wasn't very loud or enthusiastic sounding in his game, even when I told him to pick his voice up and make it fun. Most Customs officers have seen handlers acting like idiots playing with their dogs and so have a fair idea of what is expected, but the prison officers hadn't, and hence behaved with the more hushed tones and control expected of them on their rounds.

A couple of the guys, despite mentioning they owned dogs, were so wooden that Kira was quickly looking to me to play the game with her. The interviews showed up a similar lack of mental agility, with a couple of exceptions.

A former soldier who had been to East Timor had excellently prepared answers to every question, but I could see his 'boy's own' confidence could be working against him with the other interview panel members.

I really wondered whether one applicant, who laughed and answered: 'I don't know!' to several of the interview questions, had thought about it at all, and clearly he wasn't the sort of person who would be able to run his own program as the Corrections management expected.

The last officer did pick his voice up louder that the others and threw and teased Kira with the dummy fairly well, and was approved by all on the selection.

I did have mixed feelings about having another drug dog handler on the island. At least I wouldn't get so many requests from prisons, as it was one of the places I could live without. However, I knew that they would be more reliant on me, to help settle the new team in, advise them on training and they were more likely to do larger scale operations involving endless cell and shed searches, as well as start cutting my lunch on other agency jobs with the police.

It might also encourage Taspol to get their own dogs, and I would be left with little but the routine Customs tasks and no drug seizures.

Prisons had approached the Customs Regional Manager about using my supply of training drugs, but were informed with no uncertainty that they would have to get their own. I had enough problems with accounting and auditing of the stocks I had, without handing them out for use by inexperienced handlers.

Their program couldn't commence without stocks of drugs for training, and like a handler's rapport with their dog, it was something you had or you didn't, and without it, there was to be no other dog on the island.

I decided to be help rather than hindrance, and took on a role as trainer, advisor and mentor to the Corrections dog unit, finding that the selection of the last applicant interviewed had been a wise choice. He was a resourceful and determined handler who was an asset to their fledgling dog program. Working with, rather than for, Prisons expanded my role and removed any pressure about Elise's aversion to children, so the assistance wasn't all one-way.

The ex-soldier showed himself to be interested and useful in assisting the Prisons dog unit and became Corrections' second handler a few years later.

Convict country

I had managed to hop to another house sit, having met a guy from the Conservation Volunteers' office who needed someone to mind his semi-dilapidated (soon to be renovated) farmhouse, dog, cat and chooks. It was situated in the narrow, green valley of Molesworth, on the other side of the mountain from Hobart suburbs.

Molesworth is a bit of an alternative farming place, close enough to Hobart to commute in half an hour if the highway's open, but in a little world unto itself.

The police requested my help to search a property at Collinsvale, the next valley on from Molesworth. It too looked green and pleasant, but pleasant wouldn't describe the residents.

The warning signs in front of properties became more appalling the deeper one went into Collinsvale. The sign at the target address was mild – 'No through road – No visitors

– Keep out'. The neighbour was a bit more forceful, with a pictogram of a figure holding a rifle over a figure lying at its feet. 'Go ahead make my day. Turn around and f**k off', it threatened.

'Is that legal to have a sign like that?' I asked the police.

'It's considered normal up here. The closest hillbillies to Hobart.'

As a result of its convict past, Tasmania still has a strong anti-government and anti-authority streak that has continued down the generations. In convict times released convicts took up whatever opportunities arose and moved as far out of reach of the government as possible.

The jokes Tasmanians have to endure about inbreeding aren't all based on the past circumstances of geographic isolation. The standard questionnaire for pregnancy in Tasmania still asks 'Are you related to the father?' The suspect wasn't home when we arrived. While the police waited to enter the house I took Elise out to search the surrounding sheds which were full of junk, car bodies with piles of parts in the yards. Half an hour later, the owner arrived.

He kept a neat house with his chronically-ill sometime partner, and seemed to be on friendly terms with the police. I didn't enjoy his joking, smart-arse manner so I ignored his comments about my dog.

Elise had only shown a little interest in a couple of stubby holders in the bedroom that I considered could have been in contact with cannabis, so I hoped something else would be found to take the smile off our suspect's face. I had noticed a couple of flattened air rifle pellets on the floor of the shed, and during the search, the police found the air gun under a bench.

CHAPTER 9

Air guns were now considered a weapon, so they informed the suspect that they would have to take it.

Next, a handful of .22 bullets were found at the back of a kitchen drawer, but he denied any knowledge of their presence. Shortly after, a semi automatic .22 rifle was found in the garage, inside a plastic pipe with end caps that seemed destined to be buried, but had been forgotten. Again, he denied any knowledge of the rifle, claiming that due to relationship problems, he didn't spend much time there these days.

The bedroom cupboards contained many boxes of 12-gauge shotgun shells, and of course the suspect had no idea how they got there. One of the cops looked between the mattresses on the double bed, and behold – a 12-gauge pump action shotgun and a large bowie knife.

'Whose is this?' inquired the cop.

The suspect shook his head sadly. 'Never seen it before.'

'Well, you've been sleeping on it. Didn't it get a bit uncomfortable?'.

That smart-arse grin was now looking more like an idiot grin. His denials would do him little good in court. Hillbilly talk doesn't seem to cut it in the city.

CHAPTER 10

TARGET ODOURS

Members only

A national conference of dog units was being organised, and I was gratified to see that I or rather Tasmania was on the guest list. A couple of representatives from each state, well, those that had more than one handler, were being convened to discuss directions, ideas, developments, problems and experiences.

There had been a form of national meeting in June, which I heard about after it had occurred, having been called into the Customs Regional Manager's (RM) office to discuss the proposed changes to using real narcotics in public areas. I felt rather slighted, mainly because Canberra had invited other one-handler units such as Darwin to attend, and somehow we had been left out, just like Tassie was left off the map of

Australia at the Commonwealth games in 1982.

I decided to be proactive and rang the Senior Instructor in Canberra. He treated my enquiry in a very offhand manner. 'Well ... it wasn't actually a conference – just a get together of the larger units,' he claimed.

'And how does that include Darwin and South Australia?' I asked, sensing his increasing annoyance. 'I am actually asking on the behalf of the RM, who had asked me to ask why Tasmania had been excluded!' I concluded, dramatically.

There was a long silence, after which he slowly replied 'I can't tell you why that would be.'

'OK, I will pass that on, but I don't think the RM will be too happy. We'll just leave it at that this time. Hmm?'

It was a bluff, but I guessed that he would rather talk to me than the RM as they had previous disagreements. My place on these conferences, and junkets, was now assured, and it was a chance for me to feel a little bit less of an outsider.

An invitation then came from Canberra to the first Dog Unit Training Coordinator (TCO) conference in three years, with a representative from each port, including Cairns, which is a long way from Brisbane. I wasn't a TCO, but I was advising Prisons on dog training and after my last conversation with the Senior Instructor about being left out, I expected to be there as Tasmania's sole representative. I wasn't going to leave Elise out, and arranged to take her for a few days' operational experience in our previous home port Melbourne on the way back from the gab fest. A recently graduated handler in the Northern Territory was also attending so as to leave no state or territory out.

We were encouraged to arrive on Sunday night so that

proceedings could get off to a timely start on the Monday.

One of the kennel hands from the DDTC arrived to pick up Elise and me from Canberra's airport, only a little larger than Hobart's. A mini-tornado had sent trees crashing and brought down fences all around the dog-training complex in Fyshwick, smashing three cars but fortunately leaving dogs and humans unscathed.

It presented a problem. What to do with the twenty something dogs kept in the kennels? There was no longer enough secure yard space to let them all out at once. Elise would just have to wait her turn. I felt sorry for her being cooped up for three days, but as I was trying to get a couple of days' work and training in Melbourne after the conference, there was nothing that could be done.

I checked into the swanky Medina apartments on Northbourne Avenue. Canberra on a Sunday night, even a balmy summer Sunday night, was as dead as I remembered it. Apart from one pub open in Civic and some aimless strollers, there was little happening. A swanky bar on a side street, atmospherically lit with candles, had a total clientele of two.

The next day, I caught a lift into the training centre to find a scene of devastation – uprooted pine and gum trees, scattered roofing iron, shattered windscreens and crushed cyclone wire.

The conference went ahead but the presentations were interrupted by the roaring of backhoes and chainsaws outside. The conference kicked off with the question to which all other questions are secondary. What are the causes of the recent decrease in drug seizures?

Drug seizures by Customs dogs had decreased 75 per cent in the last year.

I am always suspicious of statistics and asked about the trend for Customs overall. Also down. Quantities were up but numbers of seizures were down. What changes in technology or procedures had occurred that meant that seizures normally made by dogs were being made by other means? What were the trends for the different types of drugs? Sydney has always had the most drug seizures so that team had to take much of the responsibility for the large reduction in seizures. However, it did seem that the drop in seizures was associated with greater restrictions on dog units using real drugs in training at airports due to concerns about public perception.

Unreal training means unreal expectations, and dogs can't find what they are not being trained for. Training on real drugs in realistic circumstances results in finding real drugs.

Drug traffickers had changed the business model to importing ecstasy and amphetamines instead of hash and grass, so Customs belatedly largely dropped cannabis as a target odour for dogs in order to pursue the more dangerous powder drugs. While traffickers are quick to jump on the next opportunity, changing things in government often takes years.

Elise was one of only three Customs dogs in Australia trained for all the powders and cannabis. This meant that she was suddenly getting more seizures, albeit less important ones, than dogs on the mainland. Tassie's stats were way up compared with Victoria or Queensland.

A lack of results always makes it difficult to justify costs, and the dog program was no different. The relatively low number of tasks for the FEDD dogs saw their handlers relegated mostly to a training role. A decision to give the FEDD handlers another dog trained only for cannabis would increase their workload and (hopefully) results across the board, as there were daily cannabis importations in mail that were being missed. Customs was beginning to look at putting cannabis back on the agenda.

I read with interest the Intelligence reports of the cannabis detection dogs' seizures which were distributed to all dog handlers, as were reports of all other types of seizures – powders and firearms. Until then, I didn't really think the rest of Australia was that interested in hearing about Elise's results, but I was inspired to write up her exploits. This had the effect of giving Tasmania a raised profile in people's minds. Handlers I had never met made comments such as, 'You're the guy in Tassie? You get some good hits there!'

Finding cannabis isn't as gratifying or as important as finding other types of drugs, but to a handler, finding something well hidden that would have been undetected otherwise is a validation of purpose. The dog is working as it should be.

I had thought that it would be a three-day snooze fest of debate about the various merits of passive or active responses and other technicalities, and while that was certainly on the agenda, I actually felt included, as if I was part of a bigger story, despite coming from an outpost at the bottom of Australia.

While reviewing the situation in Tasmania, I didn't pretend that I was the busiest handler in Australia. I admitted I often had to use my relationships with other agencies to keep the work coming.

We had been asked to contribute any discussion items for

the agenda, and I decided to raise the topic of whether we were still training our dogs on overly simple large odours when, as we all knew, drug seizures in real life weren't like that.

I put forward the possibility that if dogs were trained to search for more subtle odours from the beginning, then perhaps they might have more chance of success.

It was not a concept that anyone else agreed with and wasn't discussed after my long-winded explanation. Nonetheless, a couple of years later, the Dog Training centre had adopted starting dog training on much smaller odours.

As Tassie as...

Customs in Tasmania had a one-person Investigations unit as well as a one-person Dog Unit. Customs Investigations are specifically related to offences against the Customs Act that are not classed as Narcotics or prohibited Drugs. Investigation of imported drugs is done by the AFP as part of the division of responsibility made in the mid-70s when the Customs Narcotics Bureau was finally proven to be corrupt.

Pursuing the sorts of things one would be asked to declare as a passenger – weapons, medicines and pornography – are part of the role of Investigations. The division between what are classed as drugs and what are essentially medicines of a restricted nature – think of pseudoephedrine tablets which are used for treating colds but can be converted into amphetamines – is a grey area between Police and Customs investigations.

Although it didn't have direct international flights, Tasmania had a number of people using freight or mail to try to import items usually seized by Customs. Most of the mail or freight items were screened and found at the arrival ports in Melbourne or Sydney, but of course some got through.

The Investigations officer for Tassie was following up the cases of imports with particular diligence and an eye for paperwork and detail – perfect qualities for an 'Investo'. What he didn't have, fortunately, was the characteristic brashness and swagger that is so much a part of the 'Investo' culture in Customs. Because we were in Tasmania, each small section didn't have enough of its own resources, and everyone was asked to pitch in. It made for greater variety of work for Tassie officers.

A number of small mail packages from Thailand of pseudoephedrine tablets going to addresses in Launceston had been intercepted at the Melbourne mail centre, all sent from the same person multiple times. Enquiries indicated that the addresses were linked to the same man, and that the man's father was the one in Thailand sending the packages. Just keeping it all in the family.

Further enquiries with Taspol showed that the main recipient was using his mates' addresses to scatter the import of the pseudo to avoid detection. He and all of his mates also had priors for drugs and other offences in Launceston – no surprise!

Customs warrants were obtained and a joint premises search operation with Taspol's Northern District Drug Squad organised to roll all of the addresses. Customs Enforcement from Hobart and Launceston would be supporting the searches for evidence of the pseudo imports, while Taspol was providing the guns and cop attitude to deal with the locals. I was to be there with Elise with a foot in one camp and a paw in another – as a Customs officer on an Investigations warrant and as an assistant to Taspol searching for drugs. It was probably the best expression of my dual-purpose role in Tasmania.

Elise and I went up the Midland highway again to stay overnight in 'Lonny'. Elise happily curled up on the rug in front of the fire in our twee, touristy, but most importantly, dog-friendly Victorian cottage while my Customs colleagues spent a less comfortable night on the saggy mattresses of a noisy budget hotel near a truck route. The Customs accommodation budget didn't stretch as far if one didn't have a dog.

We gathered for an early briefing at Launceston Customs house, where we went over the background to the postal imports, the information on the target persons, the types of evidence we were looking for, the order of events and the combined operation with Taspol. It made a change for Customs to be leading for once and everyone was excited.

I thought it fortunate that Taspol was there because I knew that the procedures and politeness that are so much of Customs matters did not work so well when one was out of the port and airport environment and in the territory and homes of crooks. Taspol also knew all the targets, having arrested them all before, and knew them to be not the sharpest bunch but not inclined to violence.

The primary address, was near the James Boags' Brewery along the River Tamar and only a short distance from Customs House, and indeed the Police station and lockup. A look in the front and back windows confirmed that no one was home. A meeting was convened in the front car park, to the further curiosity of neighbours and passers-by on their way to work.

Customs warrants allowed a premises to be entered

regardless of whether the target was home or not, a matter usually entailing the approval of an Inspector of Police.

'No probs then,' chirped one of the police 'We've got the key!'.

With a grin the biggest copper produced a sledgehammer.

'Errr ... ahhh ... I think it would be better to call the locksmith' the Investo replied, nervously regarding the hammer. That was the difference between Customs and Police in a nutshell, really.

I sat on the tailgate of the car with Elise and chatting with the officers standing around. Shown the warrant, the young locksmith opened the door with a few clicks of a pick gun and rapidly departed.

I went in to do a safety check for Elise. Officers were standing around a computer at one end of the lounge.

'Any good?' I asked.

'Looks like everything's here,' said the Investo with some surprise.

Next to the computer were print outs of instructions on how to make speed from pseudoephedrine, emails from the father detailing how many packets of tablets he was sending, lists of the addresses and aliases used with notes of their real names, and in the bin next to the desk, empty mail packages from Thailand and empty boxes of tablets. A one-stop shop to a conviction, apparently.

'Quickest house search I've ever done' grinned the Taspol officer. 'Are all your jobs like this?'

'OK. Hold off pulling it apart until I run the dog!' I called, as there were rather too many officers of both departments in the small flat. People filed out the front and back as I brought

Elise in. Pseudoephedrine was not one of her target odours and I agreed to keep her away from that end of the lounge while they bagged the evidence. She swerved down the hall and into the bedroom, rising up on her hind legs around the built-in wardrobe. I praised her and managed to call her to search the bedside drawers of the small room before she directed her attention back to the cupboard. The door open, she pawed at a shelf of clothes and I drew her back heartily rubbing her chest while I nodded to the police to search the area. Rolls of little zip lock deal bags and packets of white cutting agent sat side by side with a scattering of cannabis.

We searched on through the other bedroom, kitchen and laundry, and knowing we had a few houses to search that day, I thought I would leave Elise hungry for more, exiting the house without giving her a dummy.

Outside, I detoured her around the police talking with a big, scruffy young bloke in an agitated state. One of the neighbours had called the owner back from his girlfriend's place.

'Warrant for what? That is bloody stupid, ya gotta be kiddin' me. Na, na ... there's nothin', youse can f**k off!' he said emphatically, shaking his head as he was led inside.

What he didn't realise was that getting hold of some packets of pseudo against regulations in Australia was a fairly minor offence, but importing a restricted product without approval and conspiracy to import were Federal charges that put him in a whole other level of trouble. He was also apparently unaware that the evidence around his computer presented a complete case against him. Even if nothing else happened on that day, he was already sunk.

There was more waiting while the Investo went over the

paperwork with the suspect. It wasn't the sort of major offence that meant offenders were placed under arrest, and the suspect was advised to attend a Record of Interview at Launceston Customs House at a later date.

On we went to the next address, predictably in Ravenswood. 'Ravo' is a hard-core public housing suburb, with a depressing amount of unemployment, criminality, drugs and violence. Sooner or later, all roads on a Lonnie drug warrant lead to Ravo.

Our line of cars into Ravo received the usual spiteful looks, yelled profanity and angry gestures. The next suspect lived at, or rather outside, his Grandmother's house, in a caravan parked in the driveway. Some of the drug squad had spotted a fellow they were looking for and zoomed off in pursuit. The Investo asked me to be one of the uniforms at the door and to assist in the hand search now we had temporarily lost some of the cops.

The caravan was locked and the elderly lady who answered the door was not forthcoming on the occupant's whereabouts.

'Whaddaya want?'

'Customs. We want to speak to the occupant,' said the Investo. 'No idea where he is. If he's not in his van, I dunno,' she grumbled.

'He's not here!' announced a young woman, appearing behind Granny with another young man in tow, apparently her boyfriend.

'We have a Customs Warrant to search this premises,' began the Investo, handing over a sheaf of papers. The older lady stared at them blankly and passed them to her granddaughter.

'Can't read this!' she said, angrily.

'I'm the reader!' exclaimed the young bloke, raising his hand and stepping forward with a grin. His brow furrowed as he scanned the pages. Minutes seemed to tick by.

'Hey, where does it say you're the cops?' he asked.

'Err … It's a Commonwealth Warrant,' the Investo pointed to the header.

'Stop usin' big words an' that!' complained the young guy.

'Well, can they come in or not?' Granny interjected

'It's to search for imported restricted items of ephedrine and pseudoephedrine,' the Investo continued.

'For what?' the girl asked.

Finally having had enough, the Taspol Sergeant stepped forward.

'It's for drugs!' he informed them.

The clouds of doubt across their faces cleared.

'Oh, why didn't ya say so. Come in then!'

They were back in familiar territory again.

The granny's house was crammed with stuff, hers and stuff belonging to the other family members that lived there. The keys were located to the caravan and the inside looked like a needle exchange kept badly, used needles and drug paraphernalia everywhere.

'Are you aware of what he's doing in the caravan?' the Investo asked the grandmother.

'Oh … the usual stuff young 'uns get up to, I s'pose,' she clucked, as if shooting up speed was just a diversion for the young.

I declined to take Elise in there, as there was too much chance of her getting a needle in the nose or paw. We did a quick run inside the house, but there were boxes, bags and piles of stuff in every room, so it wasn't very comprehensive. The Customs team did their best to search manually in the messy house and did find another couple of empty mail packages from Thailand in a bin, so it wasn't a complete waste of time.

Outside, our first suspect and a group of his mates had turned up, packed into a beaten up Ford Falcon. A policeman quickly warned them off entering the property, and as we gathered outside to move on to the next address, the Falcon took off, the occupants jeering.

The Falcon was sitting in the car park of a flat in Riverside which was occupied by the father when he was not away in Thailand sending back pills. The driver and his mates obviously had cottoned on that warrants had been issued for all the places the parcels were addressed to, and they were driving ahead to destroy any further evidence. I could see this could rapidly descend into a farce.

The flat was searched. 'Anything there?' I asked the Investo.

'Well, not any more, if there was,' he sighed.

'Can't we just pull the other warrants? This is becoming a farce with these monkeys destroying anything before we get there,' I argued.

'No, we have to execute all the warrants, otherwise I haven't completed all the components of the operation,' he insisted. The Falcon pulled out of the car park with a screech of tyres, one guy leaning bodily out of the window and screaming something unpleasant.

'OK,' I said resignedly. We drove up to West Hobart, a suburb on a steep hillside overlooking the city.

I followed the Customs and Police up a steep winding path to a large weatherboard house with flaking paint. At the top of the path, two of our friends sat on the step with a small pile of ashes smouldering on the concrete. The edge of a Thai mail parcel was still visible. They grinned smugly and laughed as we passed.

I ignored them and stepped through the entrance. The campfire boys followed and stood in the doorway, jeering.

'He he he he he ... Youse have got nothin'!' they gloated.

I turned and pointed at a large bowl of 'mull' (mixed cannabis and tobacco) on a table in the hall, apparently overlooked in their haste to destroy the postal evidence.

'What's that then?' 'Ahhh ... shit!'

Overall, it had been a successful operation for Customs, albeit a very small one, a case of the usual suspects for Taspol and a very Tasmanian experience, perhaps a case of slow and steady prevailing over making speed.

The Drug Squad Owes a Carton

On the whiteboard in the Drug Squad office was a list of names under the heading 'fines'. Fines were payable for agreed infractions of duty and the currency was beer. What one would think would be weighty matters handled badly – raiding the wrong address, losing evidence, losing equipment, letting criminals go, failing to find any drugs on warrant searches – all brought the relatively minor penalty of a six pack and a few jokes around the office. I'm sure the public wouldn't see it that way.

However, I dragged my attention away from the fines board and back to the briefing. A dealer had been calling attention to himself. A climber in the speed trade with the necessary connections to bikers, the Drug Squad had word that he was expanding his business and had even had business cards and stickers printed up, bearing a picture of his beloved motorbike and the title 'House of Speed – products to expand your mind'.

Surveillance had reported constant comings and goings at his house in suburban Lutana, but what they really wanted to know was what was going on inside. Permission to install a listening device had been granted. Clearing the house of inhabitants for the drug dog to work was a perfect cover to get the residents outside and the technicians and their bugs in, except that it usually took the techs a lot longer to do their work than it did for Elise to search the house.

The front room had been identified as the office where all the drug business was done. There was a desk, a set of scales, deal bags and a couple of ninja swords to remind the customers that the dealer was not here for fun. Taped to the underside of the desk was a dagger in a quick-draw sheath. The lounge was a litter of cannabis scraps, pills and remnants of speed deals.

The techs went in the front door as the dealer was taken out to the backyard and the drug squad guys whispered for me to stay away. Elise did her work with her usual enthusiasm and had indicated six different places around the house, including a small safe under a pile of clothes in the main bedroom. I rewarded her and then spent a long 15 minutes playing tug of war on the kitchen floor with loud exclamations to make the dealer believe we were still working.

The techs eventually shuffled out the front, shaking their heads at the barren décor they had been given to find concealment points in.

A week later, I was called to attend a briefing regarding a second visit to the dealer's house to take out the bugs and follow up on the information received. According to the Techs, the sound quality wasn't all that good, but one of the Drug Squad guys, gleefully informed me that they had heard the dealer boasting to his friends that the drug dog had been standing right next to the stash in a pot plant and hadn't done a thing.

'If we find it, you owe us a carton,' he smirked.

These sorts of comments particularly irked me and I called him on it.

'Can you tell me when the dealer, the dog and I were all in the house at the same time? We weren't. It's just one of those boasts the crooks make to sound smart to their mates,' I chided. 'Also, there are no pot plants in the house'

'Yes there are!' he argued.

'No, there are not. You'll see,' I fumed.

The house was secured again, but this time a sledgehammer had taken the front door off its hinges and it lay propped in the front hallway. The dealer sat in the backyard looking dismayed and his half-dressed girlfriend breathlessly answered questions in the lounge.

The coffee table had maybe 10 grams of grass on it amongst glasses and other paraphernalia and I told the police that I wouldn't take Elise into the lounge room at all. I was gratified to note that there were no pot plants in or out of the house.

Elise attacked a bag under the bed and indicated to several other places in the spare rooms, all of which contained containers of cutting agents or other drug associated paraphernalia. The same techs worked to remove the devices while Elise cut a fast lap around the front room, diving under the desk and coming up with a fat cannabis head in her mouth.

I pulled it from her mouth with one hand while sliding her dummy under her nose with the other. She gladly accepted the substitution and my flustered praise as I led her out. I put her back in the car and went back in to make sure that the areas I indicated were being searched.

At a loss to do anything while cameras and tape recorders were running in the house, I asked if they wanted me to search the backyard.

'No, it was done last time' was the reply. I noticed that much of the junk piled along the outside wall didn't seem to have been moved at all, and began to idly poke through it, moving items around the external pipes to see if there was any access to the walls or foundations.

Right next to the back door were bags of mulch and one of potting mix, and by the dust on the bags, they didn't seem to have been moved lately. The mulch on top was fairly loose in a clear bag but the potting mix had obviously seen a few rains and that had formed hardened layer. Still, I reasoned that the same effect could be achieved with a hose and pushed my gloved hands down into the centre of the dark brown mass, suddenly exposing gold foil underneath. I loosened the package with caution, revealing a Nobby's nuts packet containing hard lumps that were too large to be nuts and too hard to be drugs. Stolen jewellery, perhaps?

I quietly called one of the police out from the kitchen and pointed him to the gold foil. 'Hang on, we'll get photos first.' I rolled back the foil to reveal two plastic wrapped rows of 45 calibre pistol bullets.

'Didn't you say you'd searched the backyard?' I asked.

'That's a carton, mate, a carton' I crowed

CHAPTER 11

HAVE DOG, WILL TRAVEL

Somewhere in the Pacific

A couple of brief phone calls from the DDTC held out the prospect of a work trip away.

I was asked if I held a passport, just in case, not making any promises, there might be an unspecified journey in the near future. The destination, the South Pacific, was confirmed in April, but the dates were not confirmed.

Eventually official word came through that my destination was Norfolk Island.

Norfolk Island has the distinction of being more obscure than Tasmania, and more inbred. Given its small size, maybe 20 km wide by 30 km long, perhaps this is not surprising .

It was settled as a penal colony only a few months after

the landing at Sydney cove in 1788. Its second period of settlement as a punishment colony between 1825–1850 earned it the title 'Isle of Misery', a label the Norfolk Island tourism commission has been trying to put a positive spin on in recent years.

NI shares much in common with Tasmania – a convict period, failed settlements, a reputation for savagery and its appearance. A mix of rolling steep hills and valleys, it is a little reminiscent of Tasmania in parts. Certainly, the site of Kingston, with its green fields and convict settlement ruins, bears a resemblance to Port Arthur. New Norfolk, half an hour's drive from Hobart along the Derwent valley, is named for the former Norfolk Island convicts and residents resettled there.

The island is famous for being the final home of the *HMS Bounty* mutineers and their families after they left Pitcairn Island in 1856.

For weeks, I received no other news of the trip until an emailed Qantas itinerary arrived with no accompanying notes. I guessed I was going if I could make all the other arrangements.

The application for my official passport arrived at the end of the same week, and I hastened to get new passport photos and documents submitted quickly so I'd be ready for my departure from Brisbane in two weeks. It is an anomaly that one needs a passport to travel to NI from Australia, but anomalies are part of life there. NI is described as an 'Administrative Independent Territory of Australia' and is listed for government purposes as a dependent of NSW – as it was back in 1788.

Fortunately, I already had a valid passport, but the

department wanted me to travel on one with a green cover instead of blue, and DFAT obliged by sending me a new one within a week. I've always wanted to have a few spare passports, just like the scene in the Bourne identity.

One distinctive feature of Norfolk Island was that it maintained its own quarantine laws. To take Elise to NI was about the same as making arrangements to take her to the US. This was to prove a most time-consuming and frustrating process that came close to preventing me from taking her out of Australia. All the other arrangements – the dog cage, freight bookings, domestic flights, and accommodation – took a day to arrange. Satisfying quarantine requirements to take her from Australia to Norfolk Island for five days took almost as many days' work.

In the morning dark at Hobart Airport, Elise naturally baulked at going into the transport cage for the cold, dark and uncomfortable journey in the hold to Brisbane. Transferring flights at Melbourne, I saw her placed on a luggage trolley on the tarmac, wagging her tail at the passing baggage handlers in the hope that one would release her.

I knew from the bad experiences of other handlers not to board a plane until you were sure that your dog had been loaded first. On another occasion, I refused to board the flight until my dog went on as well. Despite the angst from the boarding gate staff, I knew that locating my luggage in the hold and 'bumping' me from the flight would take more time than finding my dog in the freight shed.

The plane swooped low over a green jewel of an island with tall pines like a child's drawing, Irish-green fields and scattered white houses. Seated near the front, I jumped up to be the first one out the door.

In the small terminal hall, a line of officers in pale blue shirts and neon green safety vests regarded me as I stepped forward with an outstretched hand. I guess they had me spotted as their visiting Customs officer as I had been the only single male under 50 on the plane. Norfolk's tourism appeal is mostly to the 'newly-wed and the nearly-dead', with the odd family and mother and daughter combination.

I was introduced to the chief Customs officer, a crinkle-eyed man in his fifties with a sort of smiling inscrutability about him The Brisbane flight was the first of the day, and the same plane then flew back to Sydney to bring more passengers, before returning to Brisbane again to make one more trip to NI and back. Planes arrived from Australia and NZ three days a week only, and NI Customs were keen for Elise and me to work straight off the plane, searching the same passengers we had travelled with.

I advised him that it would all depend on Elise's mood after the flight, and was handed a safety jacket to collect her from the cage being unloaded. I gave him my passport and card for processing and went to get her.

Elise was more than happy to see me and even happier to be released from the cage to run to the lush green grass at the side of the tarmac for a good sniff and a long piss. She seemed to be her usual happy self, so I walked her over to the baggage unloading area.

Elise leapt on to the pile of bags and searched feverishly – much better than I expected after the unsettling flight. I ran around the side of the trolley in the narrow garage to keep her supported as the bags shook under her. With no particular interest in any, I nodded to the unimpressed unloader and the airport fireman giving him a hand to go to work.

NI is not exactly the party destination of the South Pacific, and my role was more to screen the islanders returning home for Easter than the tourists, unless cocaine had become a treatment for angina. The officers recognised any local returning and knew their history, as people in small towns do.

'See that bloke in the red t-shirt?' whispered one.

'Oh, the guy with the walking stick?'

'No, the young bloke with the beard.'

'Yeah.'

'Get the dog around him, he's had some shady dealings,' he confirmed.

I weaved through the crowd, threading Elise between the baggage trolleys and encouraged her to search a leg her, a bag there, waving away the hands trying to pat her. 'Ohh, what a cutie!' 'Beautiful boy!' 'Sorry, I haven't got any fruit for you today.'

They weren't talking to me. I directed Elise around the red t-shirt a couple of times while he looked on with an expression of curiosity.

'How long's the dog been here?' he asked.

'Oh, a little while,' I said, reckoning that he probably knew otherwise.

Locals known for their character flaws received a full check from NI Customs, mostly uncovering undeclared food and dutiable items, but Customs didn't have powers to fine them other than taking away the goods, and the locals knew it. The side benefit of Elise's appearance was that the Quarantine amnesty bin was filled and many people had a sudden change of mind about the food question on their declarations, unsure of what the dog was searching for.

The island held about 1600 people, about 500 of whom are temporary residents and unrelated to the mutineer families, including a group of Thais brought in, not to work as chefs but to mix dough in the bakery. If one wants to become a resident of NI then it is announced in the Government notices in the Gazette, so that anyone may object.

I believe I was selected for the trip because Elise is only one of three Customs dogs trained for both powders and cannabis, and apparently the only one available at the time. It could also have been in recognition of our results in Tasmania. Elise and I had posted the largest number of drug seizures last year, but of course not of any great significance for Customs. We were the only one-dog unit in Australia and I guess Canberra thought that I could cope with working by myself.

There are many similarities and connections between NI and Tasmania in their histories. After the failed attempt in 1788 to harvest Norfolk pines for shipbuilding, Norfolk Island became a notorious penal punishment station like Port Arthur, with a model prison and other buildings similar to those on the Tasman Peninsula – a Port Arthur with pines. When the penal station closed in 1856, the remaining convicts were sent to Port Arthur to continue their torture. Their departure made NI available for the resettlement of Bounty families a few years later from the now overcrowded Pitcairn Island. The descendants of these families still make up the bulk of the NI population, with the same surnames repeated everywhere on memorials, shop names and government lists. Hence, NI has been part of an isolated society ever since Captain Bligh was cast adrift by Fletcher Christian in 1789, and has developed its own ways.

The locals speak an English dialect developed on Pitcairn between the English sailors and their Tahitian wives, and 'Island' is a pidgin of both languages, spoken with an 'Agh, pieces of eight' accent that recalls the Cornish accent of the original sailors. Of course, the islanders speak standard English to visitors, but Island between themselves.

I was privy to more 'Norfolk' spoken between the officers than most tourists. For example, I asked, 'What's happening with the ship search?'

'Hmm, I'll find out. Yeorly go lookem wuikem dar shuip, eh?' he ordered a subordinate.

'Aye,' she rolled out like a pirate. He turned to me.

'Yeah, it's happening today.'

I had picked up some rudiments of Pidgin English on a trip to the Solomon Islands years before, so I could just follow the bones of some conversations, but if they didn't want me to understand, then they just broadened their speech.

Outside the airport, I was shown to a 4WD wagon, loaded in my bags and Elise jumped happily into the back. We drove the couple of minutes down the main road lined with spiny-limbed Arucaria pines to the adjacent town of Burnt Pine, where the road was lined with duty-free shops. NI is a tax haven.

I was staying in a comfortable self-contained room at the Fletcher Christian apartments, run by Fletcher's descendants, and Elise was staying in the police cells.

Like everything, the police station was a stone's throw from the main street and manned by seconded AFP officers from

Canberra who had opted for a place to bring up their children that is quieter than Australia's capital.

Les, the white moustached Sergeant, waved off my suggestions that I could house Elise at the motel if they had some prisoners who had celebrated Easter a bit too much. 'No … it would have to be pretty bad for us to lock them up,' he said.

I was introduced to two local special constables – a geeky looking copper with skinny legs in his uniform shorts and a big rugby-built bloke with a shaved head. The cells were pretty much like kennels anyway, made for hosing down, but a bit gloomy. The police gave me a key and the door code for access anytime.

Elise was lodging just prior to NI's most infamous prisoner, due to be extradited from NZ. A young woman had been murdered on NI two years before and eventually, a New Zealander who worked there was indicted, some time after the unusual but inconclusive step of DNA testing most of the men on the island. The arrest was a great relief to the islanders, not only because the killer wasn't one of them – they would no longer have to answer the 'have you caught the murderer yet?' enquiries from tourists.

Apart from keeping Elise at the police station and borrowing some of their seized drugs for training, I wasn't doing anything – the police hadn't applied for any search warrants, despite being warned of my arrival. The balmy NI climate of consistent temperatures in the 20s, on about the same latitude as Brisbane, is ideal for growing and the green island lay as testament. No doubt it was also perfect for growing cannabis. However, the stuff seized by the police was rather poor looking and seemed to have very little smell to it. I advised them to put as much as possible around the money belt and envelopes I requested be scented for training.

My duties for NI Customs, after a signed a paper appointing me a NI officer, were to take Elise over anything coming into the island except the paper work – the passengers, baggage, freight, mail and the supply ship.

The monthly supply vessel, the *Norfolk Enterprise*, was due to arrive on its monthly supply run between Yamba in Queensland and Auckland. The ship was a smaller general cargo vessel not seen much anymore in the era of containerisation, but the facilities on the island were too limited to allow containers to be unloaded. The original convict-built wharf (1840s) at Kingston was under reconstruction, but innumerable engineering problems ruled out using that more sheltered side of the island as a port. That left the small wharf at Cascades on the northern and more weather-beaten side, under steep cliffs. The action of wind and waves interrupted the unloading – it often took two weeks to complete.

The arrival of the ship was the complete Norfolk cultural experience. Things are done in accordance with local traditions. The wharf labour is provided by Norfolk farmers who gather to do their periodic duty. Only those of Pitcairn (and hence Bounty mutineer) descent are allowed to exercise their right to work the ship.

According to the Police and Customs, part of their right involved stealing as much stuff as they could. A previous Sergeant had caught the wharfies leaving with cars full of loot, but was forced to release them when threatened that no more ships would be unloaded.

Tourist and locals come down to Cascades to watch, a reminder of the days when periods between ship visits were long. The work practices are the kind given up on the mainland in the 1970s. Gangs of men manhandle boxes into cargo nets in the ship's hold, the nets are transported to land by boat and craned up onto the wharf to be unloaded again. Ship-to-shore transport here is done by whaleboat – long wooden rowboats of the kind that were used to chase whales, although they are now fitted with engines. For large loads two whaleboats are lashed together with Norfolk pine logs and ropes to make a 'lighter' or raft, which is then towed by another boat to and from the ship.

NI Customs and I travelled out to the ship the same way as the cargo, sitting on a pallet inside a cargo net, the tension drawn up by a dock crane, which swung us down onto the lighter. Fortunately, we had the ship search training in Sydney to prepare us and Elise was happier about it than I, wagging her tail the whole way.

I had with me a backpack full of ropes and climbing equipment, but there wasn't time to use them when we got alongside the *Norfolk Enterprise*. They were eager to get us out and the cargo in, despite my misgivings about giving responsibility for our safety to a pirate gang.

The deck crane's hawser was lowered and we hopped back to the pallet, being picked up and swung onto the deck hatches, landing with a thump. I scooped up Elise by the harness and we hopped out of the net before it was picked up again. In the hold below, the crew and islanders laboured on, positioning big packs of timber to go ashore.

The Bosun was a big Tongan bloke in a too-small helmet.

He nodded a greeting and led us around the deck to sign in at the security office.

Holding only 14 crew, the accommodation block was on two levels between the engine room and the bridge. I wasn't expecting much of the search as NI Customs had no specific targets and just wanted me to help them wave the flag. I toured the decks with the Bosun and made sure all the doors were open and moved any obstacles or food lying around.

The rooms were small and didn't allow much space to search, but Elise was full of vigour, having apparently enjoyed the trip out. We squeezed past crew in the corridors and swept as space allowed around the mess rooms and stores, veering into any open cabins, while Elise sniffed the vents on any doors not open. We worked back to cover the fire equipment and electrical lockers, when Elise swung and nosed excitedly around the vent of a closed cabin door. I pushed it open and she rose up onto her hind legs, intent on the bench/bunk cabinet. A storage space under the head of the bed allowed her to stick her head in, with her tail furiously beating the air.

Until that moment I had been thinking we had probably covered enough of the ship, but I then realised that Elise was surer than I was. I drew her out of the alcove with praise and she planted her nose on the join between the woodwork and began pawing at it. I rapidly calculated that we had done all of the ship we could access and flipped the dummy out into her mouth with a resounding 'Good girl!'

While playing tug of war, I pointed out the area to be searched and pulled Elise into the security office with the dummy clasped firmly between her teeth and her tail banging the walls.

I wasn't sure how experienced NI Customs were at ship search, and anxiously made suggestions while they removed crusty clothing from the bench seat with distaste. Nothing was found, so to satisfy myself I shut Elise in the office and found that the foam bench cushion had been cut open under its cover and an obvious concealment cavity made. It was empty, but it surely had been full.

I called the Bosun to bring the crew member from that cabin up for questioning, and he shortly reappeared with a young, wide-eyed Pacific Islander who answered politely with downcast eyes.

'Know why we're doing this?' I asked

'No sir.'

'My dog says you have drugs there.'

'Oh no sir.'

'Yes, you hidem smoke in this mattress.' I held it out for him and the Bosun to see. The Bosun's eyes narrowed and he shot a question in custom language to which the crew member shook his head, miserably.

'You smoke grass, eh?' I pressed.

'No sir.'

'Does he?' I asked the Bosun.

'Not this man.'

The Bosun confirmed that the man had only signed on for this voyage a couple of weeks ago, and until then another man had occupied the cabin for nine months. If the cannabis had just been offloaded to the Norfolk Islanders, I could get Elise to search them on deck and at the wharf. I calculated that a 'smoker' may still have some saved for the weeks of possible boredom off Norfolk, and told the man he could go.

The stuff could have been moved or thrown overboard on our arrival, but it was a matter of recognising a win on a ship search – I certainly hadn't had any in Tasmania. I was pleased to have demonstrated the dog's ability, done a good job for NI and that Elise had a rewarding experience for boarding.

On our return journey in the pallet it wasn't so straight or so smooth, and I had to hang onto Elise with one hand and the cargo net with the other. The crew, no doubt, were less than happy with me after our performance on the ship. There was much muttering in 'Island' as we landed atop timber balanced across the lighter, and it didn't sound friendly.

'They're talking about dunking us in the water,' on of the NI Customs guys said.

'I reckon if it was just me, they would, but not you,' I said hopefully, watching the men closely.

'They wouldn't get away with it.' 'What would happen if they did?'

'My family would go and settle up with them, tonight,' she confirmed. Local knowledge is a valuable thing and no doubt most local disputes get settled this way and not by the police.

I had Good Friday off – no flights or ships – to explore the island as a tourist, keen to have a look around and having the benefit of a government vehicle to use.

Released from the cells, Elise jumped expectantly into the back of the car and we drove down to Kinston, the road winding down past the oldest farm settlement. It was a green idyll sloping away from a small dam. Ducks surrounded the car jostling for position, cows grazed in the lush grass and a row of tall pines lined the road.

The settlement at Kingston was very like Port Arthur,

but with the larger mansions kept in continuous use, unlike those in Tasmania. The gaping walls of the prison now looked benign and the stone convict wharf was surrounded by modern engineering attempts to make it useable. Kingston looks out onto the bare rock called Phillip Island, 10 km offshore.

At the other end of the long green lawn, across the golf course, the graveyard holds the island's past. Near the beach the lettering on the old headstones has been reworked, telling of deaths by fever, many drownings and two soldiers buried side by side who were killed by accidental discharges.

Elise sniffed happily around the historic buildings along Quality Row and flushed a brood of wild chickens flapping and squawking from a bush. I chatted with a Kiwi girl from tourist info – bumping into people is a certainty.

I took Elise on a road trip, winding along to the coastal lookout spots at all points. The northern side has steep cliffs, and the east a dramatic geological staggering of basalt columns protruding above a shell-scattered beach. In the shaded hollows the cows graze on the roadside as if arranged in rows on either side. Either the farmers choose the most traffic-conscious stock or these are the survivors.

Captain Cook landed at Duncombe Beach on the north side in 1774, claiming NI for the Crown, no doubt to stop the French claiming it for l'Empereur. Although NI is closer to French Polynesia than anywhere else, it has no transport links to it, other than through Australia or New Zealand.

I put Elise back into prison for the afternoon, so as not to break any regulations when visiting the Botanic gardens and National Park, but later found I could have taken her. From the top of Mount Pitt, only 320 m high and tarmac to the summit, one can see the whole island. The remains of the pine forests that attracted Cook's attention still reach the sea to the north and at all the other points you can see paddocks and scattered white houses dot the hilltops. It is a reminder of how small the place is, a place one would need to escape from occasionally.

Getting out of Norfolk Island almost proved as difficult as getting in, and this time it wasn't due to Quarantine. Half an hour after it left NI, the flight to Brisbane was forced to turn back with a technical issue. The island's sole aircraft maintenance engineer worked to clear it, but this would throw out the scheduled chain of flights, including my flight back to Australia. If this plane did not leave, then neither did Elise and I.

The estimations of departure times ranged from one hour to one day, depending on who one spoke to, so I went for dinner and back to the motel room to wait for the call. After a few hours of interrupted sleep, I was called to check my bags in advance, as the staff were occupied with the late arrivals.

At 2 am, I went back to the airport for the last time, my goodbyes regrettably hasty to my Customs friends. They were intent on the passengers coming in, and I on getting Elise and myself on to the flight going out as fast as they could arrange it. Of course, Elise was not pleased to be confronted by another transport cage so soon and I had to push her in for the long journey back to Tasmania.

Cairns — beautiful one day, bikies the next

Getting a working trip to Cairns was definitely a gift. It wasn't so much that the department saw me as a gifted handler, but rather that Elise was then one of very few cannabis- and powder-trained dogs and so had special skills for assisting police operations. The Queensland police knew that a bikie gang had planned a get together of their various state chapters (as the locality-based gangs are called) in Cairns. The police intended to make a show of force to send a message to the bikies.

Hobart to Cairns is a long haul, particularly with a changeover in Melbourne, making it about six hours. I watched from the terminal to make sure that Elise was loaded from one flight to the next. I never liked the thought of her stuck in a cage in the dark, rumbling hold, but as a working dog that was her role.

In the bright, hot sunshine of Cairns, she was very relieved to escape the confines and took a very long piss with an audible groan.

We were met by the Level 2 Dog Unit Supervisor, who also ran a FEDD dog, and a Narcotic Detection Dog handler.

Duties in Cairns were lighter than any of the capitals, the weather was better – except for cyclones – and the atmosphere was relaxed. Cairns had an international airport that received a few morning flights from Japan, and later in the day a few code-shared flights from Sydney and Brisbane carrying a scattering of people from Europe. Police assistance took up the rest of the Dog Unit's attention, as it did mine in Tasmania. I liked the place instantly.

Elise and I had a couple of days to adjust to the tropical conditions and, coming from the Tasmanian winter, we struggled with the heat.

The code-shared flights came in around late morning at Cairns Airport and the Customs staff, perhaps a dozen in all, were interested to see another dog working and were very enthusiastic when Elise swung and nosed the pockets of a British man walking down the aerobridge, firmly seating herself next to him before bolting away with the dummy in her mouth.

He admitted smoking hash but the 'Ionscan' (trace analysis machine) results said MDMA on his wallet. After a full search, he was let go for his holiday in the sun.

Elise got a lot of pats from the staff as I led her out of the Customs hall, happy that she was working well and we had made a good impression straight away.

The police planned to set up a roadblock south of Tully on the highway to Cairns, and give the bikies the full treatment – searches for weapons and drugs and roadworthy checks on their bikes in case they didn't get any of the former.

Tully is called the gumboot capital, due to having the highest rainfall in Australia, but not during the 'dry' season, and we drove south past the cane fields and patches of straggling tropical forests, divided with the bright green of crops. At the turnoff to Tully, a giant green gumboot adorned with a clinging frog indicated that the town's most creative minds had been at work to turn a positive out of what most people considered to be bad weather.

The brake lights of the cars ahead signaled that we had reached the lines of police vehicles on both sides of the highway. We swung over to the verge and joined the gathering around a command campervan, the sort of truck used at a big breath testing station.

There were unmarked cars positioned down the highway to report any bikies coming as well as Highway Patrol cars doing their usual job closer to Townsville further south. Until the bikies showed, the cops planned to use the opportunity to do random breath testing, roadworthiness checks, licence checks and of course drug checks on any motorists unfortunate enough to be passing. Customs had also brought their mobile x-ray van and trace analysis equipment to quickly scan any parcels or large bags.

When the bikies did turn up, the plan was for the FEDD handler to run his dog, appropriately named Siren, on the motorbikes and their riders first for firearms. I would then run Elise for drugs.

It was a long, hot day out in the sort of climate neither Elise or I were used to, so I rigged up a shade canopy over the back of the dog vehicle and kept her water bucket filled.

The police interception point on the highway was laid out like a child's toy set – pursuit cars, 'breatho' vans, prison trucks, motorbikes and lots of cops in a variety of uniforms standing around making wisecracks. Aircraft were flying around the hills on either side of the road.

'Are they yours as well?' I asked a policeman, amazed at the assets they had arranged for this operation. 'No, this is though' he pointed upwards. We were ushered back and patrol cars blocked the highway so a helicopter could land, dust and dry grass billowing out from the downdraft. It was like a scene from the Blues brothers or Smoky and the Bandit. 'Bloody hell! What next? I asked.

'They've got some tanks hidden in the grass over there,' he smiled, pointing off into the scrub. 'No, a light plane has gone down somewhere around here, so the chopper is coordinating the air search, maybe just dropping in for a social. Impressive, though eh?' he concluded. I could but concur.

The only finds I had in that long day were provided by some unfortunates in hotted-up cars and kombi vans who were pulled over out of boredom by the under-occupied cops. From the looks on the drivers' faces, they knew the game was up. When Elise responded to a cupboard in the back of the Kombi and the glovebox of the hot Commodore, she was panting so hard she barely had a grip on the dummy. It was good to give her some real rewards under such hot and trying circumstances, even if it was only on a few joints. Siren came up with some used shotgun cartridges in the back of a ute, so it was also good training for them too.

Eventually, in the afternoon, the call came through that the bikie gang were on their way.

The hollow, burbling sound of the 'hogs' announced their arrival. Big blokes, with bristly, sunburnt faces, and jaws set drew to a halt and listened silently while the QPol sergeant told them what was happening. They must have been through this any number of times. A couple of very muscular members of the Police Tactical Response Group stood either side of each man in black as they stood next to their bikes, ready to spring into action, while Siren and Elise ran around them and their bikes, careful to avoid the hot engines and exhausts.

The dogs showed a bit of interest in their bags, which were searched without result. We did about a dozen searches with the dogs before it was reported that a group of the bikies on their way up had pulled off the highway and were using a back road. Doors slammed and many Police vehicles roared off in pursuit. We waited around for a while, but then were told to stand down and packed up to return to Cairns.

The big joke was that the bikies didn't bring any drugs. They aren't dumb and of course knew that the cops would be out in force. Elise and I made the front page of the Cairns Morning Post due to a lurking photographer with a long lens.

This caused much consternation in Customs management when it was noticed. Not that the picture showed my dog working well in hot, pressured conditions, but that my shirt, the one I wear for police work with a little crest on the pocket rather than the customs logo was the wrong shade of blue. Consequently, I received a barrage of criticism from a group of suits in Canberra who have never searched a bag or dealt with an angry passenger.

Sydney — a most rewarding city (for sniffer dogs)

As the largest city in Australia, Sydney is certainly the capital for drug seizures as far as Customs is concerned, but any successes are always tempered by the knowledge that a disproportionate number of drug shipments must be getting through.

Elise and I had a good week in Sydney, not only treated with respect by the dog unit there but also treated to a number of runs on live seizures, the best training a dog can have.

Elise's identification of the drugs and performance on each one increased in steps with each successive run. I was teamed with a different handler each day around the airport and although I openly acknowledged that Elise would not be as proficient identifying the various powder drugs as the Sydney dogs, she did of course have the additional ability to detect cannabis, which their dogs were not trained for.

At Australian Air Express bond, the Customs X-ray unit believed that a roll of carpet coming from Pakistan also included some additional weave of an opiate kind. A couple of other handlers were ahead of us and a couple more were expected to take advantage of this opportunity. Handlers with experienced dogs ran their dogs around the bond and over the carpet as a 'testing' exercise to see where their dogs were at in regards to their identification of heroin.

The Level 2 Supervisor gave them little information except to run the bond. He was also in the habit of setting up such meetings in places without a drug seizure so that neither the handlers nor the dogs knew which would be a 'live' one. Handlers with newer dogs or some training problems were directed to make sure their dog had good sniffing access to the ends of the carpet rolls on a pallet and if they showed any changes in behaviour to the target roll to put them into a 'sit' and reward them. This would reinforce a stronger association with the Pakistani heroin odour as a target and make them more confident in responding without assistance.

Elise was definitely one of the latter and showed only a little interest around the pallet, possibly from the odour left by the other dogs, so rather than cue her in to a smell she didn't register, we had to leave the bond unrewarded. Fortunately, heroin isn't a commodity in Tasmania as people can just steal opium poppies from the fields.

The other runs went much better. Calls to attend DHL yielded a package sidelined by the Customs screeners suspected of containing ecstasy tablets inside books. As Elise was an 'active' response dog who pawed at articles, the box was placed behind a mesh freight box in a line of other packages opened and handled in a similar fashion. This time I left the shed smiling and Elise was woofing for joy with a dummy in her mouth. She had swung away on the first pass but stopped right on the E parcel on the second pass, inhaling deeply before raking her claws down the mesh.

The next afternoon, I was teamed up with another handler and his dog King, possibly one of the best teams Customs has ever had. Back at DHL, the screeners showed us an x-ray image of a computer monitor with a bright blue block glowing where the CPU should be. Origin – Brazil.

'Bingo – will ya look at that!' the handler smiled. He turned to the screeners.

'Don't open it. Place it down in the middle of those boxes on the floor, thanks guys!' On the first pass, DD King swung at the box and sat down hard, and the handler flicked the dummy out at his feet. An unopened box that only one other dog had been near was a gift. Elise swung out, following the phantom trail of odour emitting from the box now that a shaft of sunlight had warmed it, I turned her at the end of the row and she zeroed in on the monitor.

'Oh yes. That's how we like them. Nice and fresh. Good girl!' I cheered.

Elise's cannabis detection powers were called upon the next day. Someone had called the Customs hotline reporting buying a box of 'combusta brick' solid fuel from a warehouse that also contained a small zip lock bag of brown vegetable material.

It was a long drive to the other side of town in Sydney, and fortunately I had one of the Sydney handlers to do the driving. After several wrong turns, he found the shed in a busy industrial area. I would have been completely lost.

The Feds were waiting in the office, talking to a manager mystified as to why their Turkish fuel blocks were attracting so much interest.

'This was inside each box. Tests positive to cannabis.' The AFP officer dangled the little bag of brown blocks in front of his eyes. The manager shook his head. 'We've got most of a container load on the pallet racks. I'll show you,' he said, looking worried.

The boxes were stacked on the pallets, from the floor to above head height.

The AFP nodded to us. Gloves on, we moved a few boxes to make steps to the top of the stack.

I harnessed up Elise and gave her the 'find it!' command as soon as we were in the warehouse door, watching her carefully for the first sign of detection as the doors on the other side of the shed were open, blowing the air through.

She searched all around the stack and then over it without a flicker. I exchanged glances with the other handler. 'No alerts,' I said shortly to the AFP on our way out.

A lot of boxes were open when I came back, each with a strange little bag of brown blocks. It seemed to be a lot of effort to import some very small amounts of cannabis, and considering that they hadn't been removed from the boxes before sale, a not very effective importation.

I checked the box details. 'It says includes fire starters,' I pointed out. The penny dropped. I opened one of the zip locks and teased out the fibrous material. 'It doesn't smell like cannabis. It's hemp fibre, to use as a firelighter,' I concluded. 'It might test positive but probably isn't useable. Nothing Elise recognises, anyway.'

The manager looked relieved, and offered us Turkish tea, the Feds wondering how to deal with a case of unintended hemp product importation.

Reading the Customs summary of results a few weeks later, I saw that they had claimed it as a cannabis seizure. Even in a city awash with drugs and where Customs was making constant seizures, they were still desperate to claim a stat.

● ● ●

Our visit to Sydney also included a succession of late nights and early mornings on an airport operation. One afternoon, Elise gleefully followed a suitcase from the Lan Chile flight around the carousel and I felt that 'the mother lode' was sure to follow. I praised her and stood back to see who picked up the case.

The repetitive TV show 'Border Security' was filming inside the terminal and the director rushed over to find out what scene of conflict they could capture. I began to get a sinking feeling when I saw a mother and two kids approach the carousel. The mother lode indeed.

Fortunately, the presence of the children meant that the scene could not be filmed, and I stood behind the x-ray machine to keep out of camera range. The woman explained that the bag was her husband's, and she had left Chile and him in a hurry, bringing a black eye with her. She wasn't really sure of all the contents of the bag, but was sure that he was both an arsehole and a drug addict. The first item to be produced from the side pocket of the case was a crack pipe, so Elise was right on the money, but the search revealed little else but the sad truth of her story.

At the next bench was a guy who resembled classic

'Border Security' fodder – overweight, covered in tattoos, baggy clothing and visibly sweating. The camera team were falling over each other to stick the lens in his face. There followed an exchange so predictable I could already hear the narration that accompanies the questions about his travel, his work, his nervousness, while the machine that goes 'ping!' flashed cocaine.

The man sweated profusely as he refused to answer a question about having previously been in trouble with the police. The camera zoomed in on his face. 'Alright. I got caught with my pants down in the park, OK?' he blurted out.

I knew he had just made himself the highlight of that episode, and that Australia, and no doubt his mother, would learn his dirty secret soon.

CHAPTER 12

THE BIG SCORE

Operation INCA

In late July, Intel asked if I was available for an important job the next week 'What's it about?' I asked.'I can't tell you,' he replied, looking mysterious.

'If it's that important then I'm in.' Whatever was happening, it was obviously big, as groups of suited men and women were ushered through to the conference room for meetings that week.

The job was so big that two extra Customs NDD teams were being brought in from Brisbane a couple of days later. I arranged with Quarantine to have two kennels cleared and waited at Qantas in the afternoon for the handlers and their two black Labradors. It was a grey midwinter afternoon, and the Queenslanders' complaints about the cold started immediately outside the terminal – they'd come from mid-20s Queensland.

A few non-specific details had been released to me to assist in planning the logistics with the other handlers. For once, all Police and Customs resources were to be utilised in conjunction. Multiple premises were to be searched simultaneously, some up north, some on the East coast and in Hobart, and we would be working with separate search teams. The briefing would be given at 10.30 pm the next night, and we were instructed to arrive prepared to go immediately afterwards and to stay away at least one night.

There was snow on top of Mt Wellington, a phenomenon the Queenslanders hadn't experienced before. It was a pleasure to watch them experience the first thrill of walking in, tasting and throwing snow like children, their dogs uncertainly sniffing at it and walking gingerly on paws unused to cold.

The origin of the operation was the AFP so they were acting as warrant holders while Taspol officers acted in support – an interesting exercise in co-operation – or the lack of it – at all levels.

In the Drug Squad lunchroom late that night, the details were released to our expectant ears by the team of detectives and senior officers.

Operation INCA had begun with the investigation of Mafia drug importations into Australia and been galvanised by the (as yet) unannounced seizure of four and a half tonnes of Ecstasy (E) tablets in Melbourne. The pills had arrived in a shipping container of cans of tomatoes from Italy, but the drugs had originated in the Netherlands. Apparently they were worth $10 million wholesale and perhaps $100 million on the street. Few criminal organisations had the money to purchase that quantity of drugs, let along the structures to distribute it and the guns and muscle to protect it.

The seizure had been kept quiet while Customs and the AFP tried to affect a 'controlled delivery' – substituting most of the drugs with a benign placebo, in case something went wrong, while leaving enough of the real thing in the shipment to qualify for an 'importing a commercial quantity of a prohibited substance' charge. In this case, 500 kg of E was left in while hundreds of thousands of placebo pills were rapidly produced as a secret special order, then sealed in look-alike cans.

The container was then wired up with bugs and trackers to follow its onward passage after the container was replaced on the wharf. The trap was set.

No one appeared to collect the container, despite some anonymous enquiries made to the shipping company to try and get it delivered, but in the meantime the AFP followed all leads looking for the sort of activity that abandoning a huge shipment of drugs would create. It was a business crisis in anyone's terms, and would also involve a subsequent scramble to try and rapidly replace the loss by the criminal networks involved.

The main target was a Mafia kingpin in Melbourne already suspected of involvement in many previous drug importations, but never one this big. He usually stayed at arms length and that had kept him out of court so far.

Six months had gone by while all the leads were followed on the container of MDMA and it was now time to act. twenty five warrants were to be executed simultaneously in Australia and another three overseas.

The target I was assigned had a property on the East coast, and another on a river in the north. His distribution network was limited to a couple of people on the East coast and Hobart and they were the targets of other teams. It wasn't clear which property the target would be in the next morning, but the SOG were in position around both and the phones were tapped, so he was boxed in either way.

The warrant teams would travel in convoy, leaving immediately and assemble at RV points before moving up to standoff positions near the properties, where the SOG would let the commanders know what the situation was.

I put Elise in the AFP station wagon and we drove into the night at standard police speed – well over the speed limit. Eventually we pulled over behind a Drug Squad car. Over the next half hour we were joined by various other officers – forensics, photographers and uniforms.

It was a cold night and I pulled on a beanie and gloves while two forensics officers fired up a camp stove and everyone huddled around coffees. Only the dogs didn't seem to mind, but I was sure the Brisbane teams would be suffering.

When it was time we headed off in convoy.

I was glad I wasn't driving on that twisting, foggy, animal-crossed road as my instinct to stab the brakes would have left us far behind the convoy, but our driver had been trained as a pursuit and VIP escort driver and kept the hammer down. Our headlights lit up a circle of people in a car park, muffled in coats while an AFP officer tried to get an aerial up on the roof of the information shelter.

It was raining and didn't look like stopping, the sky black

and broken only occasionally by a suggestion of moonlight.

'Bugger of a night to be crawling around the bush,' I observed.

'Ah, the 'Soggies' (Special Operations Group) will be loving this,' was the consensus from their colleagues. Soggy, indeed!

The satellite phone wasn't working for some reason, and nor was the other emergency phone despite the extra aerial, so communications were very limited to the base and all the other teams. A couple of the forensics cars hadn't turned up, but there was no way of contacting them, so the AFP team leader decided we should move up to the form up point just short of the property. It seemed that the slick, high-tech international police operation was breaking down into something a little more Keystone cops for the Tasmanian part. After giving Elise time for a leak, we joined the rear of the convoy again.

Along a dirt road, a succession of brake lights and long stops told us that the AFP weren't really sure where the turn off to the property was, having only seen it in daylight once. During that visit, they apparently forgot to GPS it so it could be found in less clement conditions. We turned down one muddy track after another, the wheel ruts filling up with water, the lead car U-turning with the whole circus slowly following.

Eventually we pulled up near a gatepost on which a glowstick lay.

The car lights were turned off and we took care to close the doors softly, even though many of the other cops did not.

'Aren't the SOG meant to be here?' asked someone. There was the sound of movement and a torch beam swung onto a walking tree, like an extra for Lord of the Rings. A bough lifted and pulled the shaggy crown back, revealing a savage grin underneath a moustache and a face smeared in camouflage paint.

'How are yas?' grunted the tree, shifting an M-16 with a night vision scope from under a cape of scrim netting. Perhaps more Apocalypse Now than Lord of the Rings.

'Yep, the soggies are loving it,' someone muttered.

I went and sat on the wagon's tailgate while the SOG conferred with the commanders, and after another 10 minutes was called to join the gathering. The bad news was that our target was not at this property. However, a listening device placed under the floor confirmed that his wife was at home. Rather than create unnecessary conflict with a crash-bang 'hard entry' to the house, the police decided to call her on the phone and ask her to come out. The warrant holders left us listening to the patter of the rain, croaking frogs and odd startled cry of the lapwings while they walked up the long driveway with the SOG.

Another 15 minutes ticked by, broken by a loud rushing sound and an explosion of light in the sky, welding-torch bright and crackling as it swayed down, trailing smoke. The shadows leapt around as if all the trees were now walking. I gasped and stared transfixed, waiting to hear shots. None came.

'What does that mean? I asked the police, in the absence of any other comment.

'Dunno'

'Well is it good or bad?' I persisted. There was a flat 'crack!' sound and another flare burst in the sky.

'Is two better?' I asked. No one answered. The radios were still silent No one knew what was happening.

'I reckon the Soggies had a whole lot of flares to use up'

someone said.

A radio crackled. 'All clear. Come up!'

The house stood in a clearing in the scrub, illuminated by many headlights. A caravan and a couple of cars, neither new, sat under a carport. A circle of cops stood around a woman in a dressing gown and led her away from the door. The entry teams went in to check no one else was inside. While I waited at the car, I put on my headlamp and checked out the yard, scattered with well-tended plants, little statues and furniture. Opposite was what looked like another house, which hadn't been mentioned in the briefing. I grabbed my large Maglite and started carefully towards it, playing the light over the water tank and haystack around it. A bush suddenly rose up before me and I jumped.

'G'day,' muttered the bush, tucked an M-16 under its arm and rustled off into the darkness. Best to stay at the car until the police had finished their bit, I guess.

When Elise and I got inside the house we found the layout was basic – a large back room filled with tools and outdoor furniture, three bedrooms and a large kitchen and lounge.

The interior decoration was fussy – faux farmhouse furniture with lots of feminine touches of gingham, embroideries and rag dolls. It would have been freezing inside if the two wood stoves weren't going.

Elise worked fairly well despite the odd hour but didn't show any interest in the kitchen and lounge. I praised her and took her back outside.

The caravan looked as if it hadn't been used recently and was full of old kitchen stuff, clothes and books. Elise showed no interest in the van or the Ford Falcon parked next to it. I had thought that she might react inside the car if it had been used to transport the E tablets over on the ferry, but she gave a close search without any change in behaviour.

The shed was piled with the remnants of farm life – tools, plastic pipes, rusting bits and pieces, engine parts, fuel drums, torn shade mesh, tyres and broken stuff from the house. We stepped around and over the piles, checking for anything that could hurt the dogs, moving open fuel containers, broken glass, saw blades and rat poison out of the way.

Elise was distracted in the yard, nosing around the wallaby poo and the chook pen at the back of the shed – interesting smells for a dog – but I wasn't sure that she had her mind on the job of looking for drugs.

To encourage her, I picked up my voice and animated my movements, but I knew that it would be a difficult task with so much to search. Elise responded well, charging into the shed with vigour and exploring the varied smells of the new area with interest, working fast and pulling ahead on the lead so that I had to quicken my steps to direct her on to the next feature. I concentrated on navigating around the shed while trying to keep an eye on where we had searched and where we hadn't – not that easy when you're watching the dog.

Her tail began wagging before she cast back and forth in a corner, stopping dead on a white plastic bucket sitting on top of a pile of grain sacks. Her paws launched it against the wall before I began to reel her in. It was obviously empty – there was still much to cover.

We worked on and she swung again at the bucket (which I'd placed on a bench) as we left. I gave Elise some more praise and a rest outside. We started searching again, circling her around the outside of the shed to search other piles of junk and lean-tos. It was still raining and my pants and boots were dripping wet.

All the other police, except one AFP officer, had withdrawn to the house – we were the only idiots out in the rain.

'Should Narcotest that container,' I said to myself. At least it would give the dog and me a break before dealing with the rest of the property.

I retrieved some swipe tests in their foil packs and applied one to the inside of the bucket, dunking the test strip in water for a few seconds. In a couple of minutes, the test showed a tell-tale red stripe in the MDMA section.

'Hey … it's positive!' I held the test out to the AFP officer.

We took in the crowded shed. 'What do you want to do?' he asked. 'Well … look around nearby. I'll start here,' I said, indicating the area where the bucket was found.

'I'll start here' he said, stepping to a couple of plastic bins of chicken feed on a pile of junk across from me. I tossed him a pair of plastic gloves from my pocket.

'I've found heaps of stuff in these before,' he reminded me of his experience with Queensland Police. He pushed his hand down into the grain.

'Jesus!' he exclaimed and pulled his hand out. 'There's something in there.'

I bounded over to him and scrabbled down into the bin while he tilted it. I found the top of a clear plastic bag and pulled. A couple of thick wads of hundred and fifty dollar notes emerged from the feed.

'Oh Yes! We've got him!' I cried. I handed the cop the bag and burrowed down to the bottom. A bulky package wrapped in grey plastic supermarket bags lay there. It seemed to be a piece of electrical equipment.

'The heat sealer, you reckon?' the AFP officer asked. We tipped all the grain out before turning to the other bin. I grabbed a stick and pushed it down into the grain. It stopped halfway down. We exchanged glances and the officer stepped towards the door to get the photographer.

The Drug Squad left the warm house and helped me smooth the grain off the top to reveal another white plastic bucket with a lid. When the lid was prised off, I saw a crush of plastic bags. The one at the bottom bulged with green diamond shaped tablets. I held the bag up.

'Elise, you beauty!' I shouted. Smiles all round.

'Better put it back for the photos' someone said. It was put back and the grain poured back on.

It wasn't a straight dog hit – the dog indicated a spot and drugs were found there, but if it hadn't been for Elise's interest in the bucket, I don't think it would have been found.

We stood outside the shed while the photos were taken. The Drug Squad's conversation turned to which one of them was going to claim it as 'their' hit. So much for inter-agency cooperation.

We went back to the search. One of the forensics officers with not much to do came in to help us. On a high shelf, he found a paint can that contained used zip lock bags, apparently used packaging for Ecstasy, according to the Narcotests.

Why the suspect had kept them, I have no idea. It seemed like he had become complacent and decided that he wasn't likely to have a visit from the police anytime soon. The storing of the drugs and money so close together, and so close to the house when he had a huge area to hide it in smacked of laziness, thank goodness.

It was raining harder, and the cold and wet would not be helping to make odours rise to be available for the dog. In those conditions, we were more likely to find something by visual indicators, so we left the dog in the car and went for a long, wet walk. We poked through haystacks, chicken coops, car bodies and tree stumps, then followed the bush tracks in a rough circling of the property.

After disturbing a few wallabies and getting even wetter we headed back to the house.

In the kitchen, the tablets (about 3000 or 1.8 kg) and the cash were laid out on long strips of brown paper in equal piles, surrounded by a respectful circle of police taking stills and video while the numbers were announced for the purposes of the tape.

What I really needed was a toilet break and a hot drink, so I interrupted the proceedings to inform them we had done as much as we could outside. Once again, I felt that the dog really had made a difference. Incredibly tired but elated, I joined my driver for the drive back to Hobart. I realised with a jolt that this was the day Elise and I had been working towards our whole time in Tasmania.

I called the Hobart office and told them the good news. We shared stories over a beer at Customs house. Elise was back in her kennel with a big bone to gnaw on.

I received recognition in Customs for the hit.

Much appreciated was a call from the Taspol Drug Squad. 'I heard Elise found the goods?' my caller began.

'Yes, indicated in the area and the drugs and cash were

found by a joint effort with an AFP officer,' I confirmed.

'Yep, just wanted to get it straight from you before any tales get told around here,' he replied. It was a vindication of his trust in Elise and me and I was glad to pay that trust back with interest.

A couple of months later I was invited to a debriefing for Operation INCA. Two of the main AFP investigators from Melbourne had put together a presentation to explain how all the pieces fitted – and it made a bizarre puzzle.

Tasmania received a special mention for seizing the 3000 ecstasy pills, which had been part of a later 'tagged' shipment intercepted and let run through to known distributors. It was the largest MDMA seizure in Tasmanian history – so far – and I was proud that Elise and I had played our part.

At a national video conference, I received recognition for the INCA seizure and gave due credit to all colleagues involved, mentioning that I could only represent it as a symbol of co-operation.

Elise and I had just had our best day at work. As someone later reminded me, 'At least you know you've had one, most people never do!'

CHAPTER 13

THE LAST PARADE

Old dogs

I frequently had enquiries from people asking what happened to Customs dogs when they retired, many having the idea that, unwanted for service, they might be put down. I was always able to reassure them that only rarely are the dogs not taken by their handler, puppy walkers or Customs staff to live out retirement in comfort, often with retired officers.

Hobart Customs house hosted its annual Retired Officers night a couple of weeks before Christmas. The murmur of conversation and the clink of glass carried from the amenities room. Inside, a collection of white and grey-haired men chatted in small circles with the current staff scattered throughout.

I just had time to get a beer before the social organiser tapped his stubby to signal for quiet. 'Welcome, everyone!

How good it is to see familiar faces, but sadly the gathering has shrunk over the years,' he remarked.

'Speak for yourself!' chirped a small man with a wizened face and a prominent gut.

I spoke to two officers about the old days when Hobart was a thriving commercial port full of cargo ships from all over the world collecting Tasmanian apples for export. They reminisced about how hard they had to work. When they needed a break they had the switchboard girls worded up to send any calls to the pub, where they answered, 'Customs House'.

Awaiting arrivals at Beauty Point out of Bell Bay in the north, there was time for fishing and drinking, disturbed by occasional bouts of form stamping and checking whenever a ship carelessly decided to dock. Boarding the ships, a job that now requires carrying a gun, meant two or three hours of solid drinking with the Captain while the paperwork was done.

When I joined Customs in the 1980s meal times and often tea breaks were spent at the pub. Many of the older officers bemoaned not being able to smoke at their desks anymore. At the airport, this included smoking at the arrivals desks while stamping passenger's passports.

Framed pictures on the wall showed many of those old men as slick haired boys with jutting ears and Adams apples, their peers smiling into the camera from another era.

Times have changed!

Lest we forget

I was asked whether I'd received an invitation to the Army tracker dogs' parade in March. I hadn't, but soon received a call from the Army Tracker Dogs Association, a Returned

Servicemen's association formed by Vietnam veterans of the Army's first tracker dog teams.

They had developed a memorial walk in a park at Berriedale in remembrance of the dog teams and especially of the dogs, handlers and support team members that didn't return.

The ex-serviceman asked me if Customs could attend the ceremony, as they were trying to get a number of canine representatives from all services to give the occasion an air of relevance to dog handling in general. I said I would be happy to attend.

'How many of you do you think could come?'

'Well I'm it in Tasmania, the only one.'

I had picked up the book 'Trackers' (Haran, P. New Holland Press) at the War Memorial during my time in Canberra. The subject was the dog teams in Vietnam. Military history has always interested me and I was surprised to find a book on this specialist field.

Trackers details the experiences of a soldier in training and in action in Vietnam, leading patrols while his black Labrador pointed out hidden Vietcong positions. They didn't work alone of course, but operated ahead of the main forces. Each dog team was followed by a support team of three to five men with heavier weapons like machine guns and grenade launchers. It wasn't work I would care for.

The army dogs in Vietnam were not trained to find explosives but saved their handlers many times by pointing to where mines had been laid, I presume because they could detect the human odour left by enemy mine layers.

More recently the army have used firearms and explosive search dogs very successfully in Somalia, Bougainville, the

Solomon Islands and East Timor to support operations to disarm combatants. The ability of Army dog teams in Iraq and Afghanistan to locate IEDs and weapons caches has been a critical tool in combating those insurgencies.

I went down to Berriedale Park the day before the ceremony to check out the memorial. The bayside pathway was marked at intervals by totems describing Australian Service dogs in conflicts from the First World War to East Timor, giving the known names of the dogs and a short description of their duties. On the other side of the path were memorial trees to the Vietnam tracking wing handlers, trackers and support team soldiers who were killed in action.

The sad thing about the service dogs was that unlike their handlers, they were not returned to Australia due to the army's refusal to pay the quarantine fees. They were generally given to local families as pets and their fate after the Communist takeover in 1975 remains largely unknown.

A descriptive board was placed at each end of the path explaining service dogs and the purpose of the memorial, and at the head of the bay a small memorial garden with dedications had been carefully made. Much time, work and energy had gone into making this symbol of esteem for working dogs.

The ceremony was to occur on a Saturday afternoon and fortunately the day was warm and sunny, not a given in Hobart even in summer. The Police pipe band were kitting and kilting up, a squad of cadets checked their uniforms and a loose knot of older men with rows of medals circulated. I parked to one side and got Elise ready as the pipe band started forming up.

The veterans moved into ranks behind the band, and asked

that the dogs be at the front of the parade behind the band. The police escort arrived and the band struck up 'The British Grenadiers' as they swung out onto Main Road.

I walked Elise along. She wasn't used to walking to heel on her choker and continually pulled ahead, being used to leading. Fortunately, it wasn't far down the road and we stepped along to where the dignitaries and families waited, an Army honour guard standing with heads bowed. A plaque was unveiled to applause and the Last Post played with its sobbing notes of sorrow, prayers offered for the fallen and the dogs left behind.

I waited after the ceremony while people came up to pat Elise, a sort of cuddly relief after the service. A white-haired man leaning on a cane leant down and crooned to Elise, who gladly licked his face.

'Mine's gone,' he said sadly, and slowly rose and limped away.

Lest we forget.

POSTSCRIPT

NDD Elise and I started our life in Tasmania as the only drug detection dog team in the state. Changes in policy meant that Elise was to be the last Customs dog in Tasmania.

Her life came to an end in a sudden and unexpected way. In May 2009, Elise suddenly developed an aggressive abdominal cancer. After emergency surgery, Elise managed to return to work for a few months before ill health forced her retirement. She spent her last few weeks with me at home. She was given goodbye ceremonies by Customs, AFP, Taspol, and Tas Prisons.

The day before her final trip to the vet, we lay on the deck in the sun, under Mt Wellington, her head resting on my chest. It was Elise's last, beautiful day on earth. She is buried in our garden.

I was re-teamed with NDD Cougar, a male black Labrador with liquid brown eyes and a gentle nature. I had handled him in Canberra during the training course in 2004, where I was subsequently teamed with Elise.

Customs decided to close the Tasmanian Detector Dog Unit in 2011. Cougar was retired, along with me. He enjoyed his retirement, turning all his drug detection capabilities to finding food, a true Labrador pursuit.

Meredith and I decided to stay in Tasmania and I became a full-time parent, looking after our son. It was a very outdoor upbringing and together we walked Cougar twice a day, every day.

Cougar died in 2016, and is buried next to Elise, the last Customs dogs on the island.

GLOSSARY

AAE	Australian Air Express- air cargo company
AAD	Australian Antarctic Division
ABS	Air Border Security, Customs tarmac team
ACS	Australian Customs Service, now Border Force Australia
Active response	pawing at a target odour
AFMA	Australian Fisheries Management Authority
AFP	Australian Federal Police
ANARE	Australian National Antarctic Research Expedition
APS	Australian Protective Services, government security guards
Aereolineas	Argentinasnational airline of Argentina
ASIO	Australian Security Intelligence Organisation
CET	Contraband Enforcement Team, Customs cargo search team
CIB	Change in Behaviour, a dog showing interest but not an obvious alert
CO	Central Office, Canberra
Connie	Police constable
CPSU	Community and Public Sector Union
CPU	Central processing unit of a computer
CT	Counter-terrorism
Customssee	ACS
CWDD/Chem.	Chemical weapons detector dog
DAS	Dept. of Admin Services, federal government logistics
DD	Detector Dog
DDTC	Detector Dog Training Centre
DDU	Detector Dog Unit

Deal bags	small zip lock bags for holding small amounts of drugs
DHL	Airfreight express courier company
DSG	District Support Group, Vicpol area special duties group
Dummy	A rolled towel retrieval toy reward
E, Eccy	Ecstasy or MDMA amphetamine substance
EDD	Explosives detector dog
FEDD	Firearms and Explosives detector dog
Fedex	airfreight express courier company
GP	General Purpose (police) dog- tracking and attack
Grass	Cannabis
HAP	Hobart Airport
Hash	Cannabis resin
Hit	Seizure of drugs or other contraband
Ionscan	Trace analysis device for drugs and explosives
Itemiser	Trace analysis device for drugs and explosives
Lan Chile	national airline of Chile
Level 1/2/3	Customs ranking system, 1 being the lowest.
MAP	Melbourne Airport
MC	Motorcycle Club (gang)
MHU	Mail Handling Unit, Australia Post facility for moving mail
MPR	Multi-Purpose Response, dog trained to paw at articles and sit next to people
Muttluks	protective boots for dogs
MXU	Mobile x-ray unit for Customs
Narcotest	chemical reagent kit for drug testing
NCA	National Crime Authority
NDD	Narcotic Detector Dog
NI	Norfolk Island

NM	National Manager
NSWPol	New South Wales Police
OMCG	Outlaw Motor Cycle Gang
PAD	Passive Alert Dog, a sit response to a target odour
Pseudo	Simulated narcotics, having a similar odour but without drug effects
QPol	Queensland Police
RM	Regional Manager
SAP	Sydney Airport
SAPol	South Australian Police
SOG	Special Operations Group, police SWAT team
SOMPRU	Southern Ocean Marine Patrol & Rescue Unit, Customs sea patrol
Speed	Amphetamines
Spirit of Tasmania	Melbourne to Devonport ferry service
Smack	heroin, opiates
Stim	Eliciting stimulus, a target odour, set up as a training exercise
Sub	Substitution of a reward toy for a target odour
Supervisor	Customs Level 3
Taspol	Tasmanian Police service
TCS	Tasmanian Correctional Services, Tas prisons
Team leader	Customs Level 2
Toll	sea cargo company
TRS	Tourist Refund Scheme
ULD	Unit Lifting Device- a stackable transport cage
UPS	air express freight company
Vicpol	Victoria Police Service
WMD-	Weapons of Mass Destruction

ABOUT THE AUTHOR

Steve Kelleher worked as an Australian Customs Dog handler for 16 years, including six years in Tasmania. He has travelled extensively and studied nature conservation while attempting to become a park ranger.

Steve has an appetite for good stories and believes that a journey isn't over until the stories about it have been written. He also believes that work is a long and often overlooked journey.

He was a full-time parent for three years, until taking up a dog handling position recently with Biosecurity Tasmania. Steve still lives in and loves Hobart.

First published in 2017 by New Holland Publishers Pty Ltd
London • Sydney • Auckland

The Chandlery Unit 704 50 Westminster Bridge Road London SE1 7QY
United Kingdom
1/66 Gibbes Street Chatswood NSW 2067 Australia
5/39 Woodside Ave Northcote, Auckland 0627 New Zealand

www.newhollandpublishers.com

A record of this book is held at the British Library and the National Library
of Australia.

ISBN: 9781742579603

Group Managing Director: Fiona Schultz
Publisher: Alan Whiticker
Project Editor: Bill Twyman
Designer: Andrew Quinlan
Production Director: James Mills-Hicks
Printer: Hang Tai Printing

10 9 8 7 6 5 4 3 2 1

Keep up with New Holland Publishers on Facebook
www.facebook.com/NewHollandPublishers